THE FOUNDATION OF ALL GOOD QUALITIES

THE FOUNDATION OF ALL GOOD QUALITIES

A Commentary on the Verses of Lama Tsongkhapa

By Geshe Tsultim Gyeltsen

Based on an Oral Translation by Losang Gyaltsen

THUBTEN DHARGYE LING PUBLICATIONS

THUBTEN DHARGYE LING ARCHIVE
P.O. Box 90665 • Long Beach, California 90809 • www.tdling.com

© Geshe Tsultim Gyeltsen 2006

ISBN: 0-9623421-7-3

For free distribution
Published by Thubten Dhargye Ling Publications

Cover Art:
Painting of Lama Tsongkhapa with kind permission
Himalayan Art Resources website • www.himalayanart.org
Front cover background design with kind permission from
Robert Beer. From *The Encyclopedia of Tibetan Symbols and Motifs*;
Shambhala Publications, 1999.
Back cover photo by Don Farber

Cover & Book design by Gopa & Ted2, Inc.

Table of Contents

Acknowledgments

THIS BOOK HAS BEEN MADE POSSIBLE through the effort and commitment of a number of individuals. First of all, we would like to thank Losang Gyaltsen who contributed a profound and accessible translation of the oral commentary from Tibetan into English. He has translated for Venerable Geshe Gyeltsen many times in the past, and we greatly appreciate his dedication, skill and humility. The English translation of this teaching was transcribed, edited, and prepared for publication by Rebecca McClen Novick. Geshe Gyeltsen went over the text with meticulous attention to make corrections and to clarify certain topics. Any errors in the text are solely the responsibility of the editor. We would like to thank Bhikshuni Tenzin Kacho for inviting Geshe Gyeltsen to give these teachings in Colorado and thus for making this publication possible. We also thank Venerable Gyalten Thartso for ensuring that the teachings were recorded so that others could benefit from them. We are also extremely grateful to Doren Harper for his devotion to the mission of Thubten Dhargye Ling's Archive Project to preserve and disseminate teachings such as these and for his generous assistance with this project. We extend our thanks also to Annie McCormack for her administrative assistance and her tireless efforts to ensure the success of all Geshe Gyeltsen's projects. Thanks also to Gopa & Ted2, Inc. for their beautiful layout and design, to Dr. Nick Ribush for sharing his experience, and to Tenzin Dorjee for clarifying many points of dharma. Our deepest gratitude is reserved for the author of these teachings, Venerable Geshe Tsultim Gyeltsen, for his great kindness in giving the oral commentary, for his supervision of the project, and for remaining as a luminous example to us all.

:: Foreword

IN JANUARY 2006, Venerable Geshe Gyeltsen traveled to Colorado at the invitation of Bhikshuni Tenzin Kacho and the students from Thubten Shedrup Ling in Colorado Springs. For three days, Geshe Gyeltsen gave intensive instruction on *The Foundation of All Good Qualities* to about forty students, old and new, in a remote mountain retreat. *The Foundation of All Good Qualities* is a very condensed lam-rim text by the fourteenth century Tibetan master, Lama Tsongkhapa. Everyone was very engaged and attentive while Geshe Gyeltsen offered a thorough and many-layered explanation of the text, which although only fourteen verses long, contains the entire stages of the path to enlightenment from the significance of guru devotion to the entering of the tantric path. Losang Gyaltsen traveled from San Francisco to act as translator for these teachings, and a number of Geshe Gyeltsen's long-time students traveled over the Rockies from Western Colorado to attend. For some, it was their first Buddhist teaching retreat, but no matter whether the students were new or experienced, all those present found this teaching very profound. It was felt that to make this teaching available in book form would be extremely helpful to practitioners of all levels. Thus the decision was made to publish this book through Thubten Dhargye Ling's Archive Project for free distribution, in the belief that the dharma should be accessible by all. The students of Geshe Gyeltsen are very pleased to be able to offer this book in honor of the September 2006 visit of His Holiness the Dalai

Lama to Los Angeles. May all those who come across these pages find true happiness for themselves and others, and may all beings everywhere benefit from the positive energy generated from those who read and practice these precious instructions.

THE FOUNDATION OF ALL GOOD QUALITIES:

A Commentary on the Verses of Lama Tsongkhapa

by Geshe Tsultim Gyeltsen

Lama Tsongkhapa

Root Text

1. The foundation of all good qualities is the kind guru.
   Cultivating the guru properly is the root of the path.
   Realizing this clearly, with great diligence,
   bless me to rely on the guru with highest devotion.

2. Only once won this glorious birth of freedom.
   By appreciating its rarity and meaningfulness
   with a mind that seizes its essence day and night,
   bless me to generate this thought continuously without cease.

3. The motion of body and life force is like a bubble, swiftly perishing.
   Therefore, contemplate impermanence,
   for after this life, just as shadow follows form,
   good and bad karmic fruits pursue us.

4. With this firm conviction,
   abandoning even the smallest non-virtue
   and engaging in every virtuous deed,
   bless me to always live conscientiously.

5. Samsaric splendors are never satisfying,
   they are unreliable and the door to all misery.
   Seeing these faults, for the joy of Nirvana,
   bless me to generate intense enthusiasm.

6. Inspired by this immaculate determination,
   with mindfulness, alertness, and great conscientiousness,
   bless me to pursue the pratimoksha vows— the root of the teaching,
   as my core practice.

7. Just as I have fallen into the ocean of samsara
   so too have wandering motherly beings.
   Seeing this, bless me to develop the altruistic mind
   that assumes the responsibility to free them all.

8. If this resolve is created
   yet habituation in the three ethics is lacking,
   enlightenment cannot be achieved.
   Realizing this fully, bless me to train in the
   bodhisattva precepts with strong enthusiasm.

9. That which prevents distraction towards distorted objects
   and enables analytic penetration into the perfect meaning,
   bless me to quickly produce in my mindstream
   the integrated path of shamatha and vipashyana.

10. When I am well trained in the common paths
    and have become a proper vessel
    for the Vajrayana— the pinnacle of all vehicles,
    bless me to effortlessly enter
    this gateway of all fortunate beings.

11. Having discovered with unyielding conviction
    that the ground for attaining two forms of siddhis,
    is purely observing the vows and samayas,
    bless me to safeguard these more than my life.

12. *Having realized the quintessential points*
of the two stages—the heart of all Tantra,
and unwavering from four daily yoga sessions,
bless me to practice according to the words of the masters.

13. *May the gurus, the beacons of the perfect path,*
and faithfully striving companions have long life.
May hosts of obstacles, external and internal,
all completely subside.

14. *In all my lives may I never be apart from perfect teachers,*
and fully enjoy the magnificent dharma.
By attaining the complete realizations of stages and path,
may I swiftly attain Vajradhara's state.

Introduction

I BELIEVE THAT ALL SENTIENT BEINGS down to the smallest insects all share the same wish—to get rid of suffering and find happiness. In that regard, we as sentient beings are all the same. However, when we look closely, we see that our lives do not match the wishes we have for ourselves. Although we do not want suffering, we encounter suffering in many different forms, and although we wish to have happiness, most of us are deprived of true happiness.

The reason for this is that most of us are ignorant about all the negativities and mental defilements that we need to get rid of, and the positive actions and qualities that we need to cultivate and adopt. Also, even if we have a certain understanding of these things, we are not putting what we know into practice.

The solution to ignorance is the acquisition of knowledge and understanding. This involves educating ourselves about the teaching and practice of Buddhadharma. We have to study the original teachings of the historical Buddha, which are contained in the sutras, as well as the commentarial treatises written on Buddha's teachings called *shastras*. It's through education, through study, and through listening to teachings, that we remove ignorance from our mind. Listening to teachings kindles the light of wisdom within us that dispels the darkness of ignorance. This is why the Buddha emphasized the benefits of listening to dharma teachings.

We might think that it's a waste of our time to spend years studying the dharma. We want to practice meditation right away because we that think this is how we'll get closer to enlightenment. But the fact is that listening to teachings is absolutely crucial to our understanding of dharma or spirituality. Without listening to the dharma we will lack discriminative awareness. We won't be able to distinguish between what is spirituality and what is not spirituality; between what we should and should not do. If we randomly try to engage in a practice without first becoming educated about it, we are not going to get very far. As it is said, "Trying to practice without listening to teaching is like a handicapped person trying to be a rock climber."

Without study, we cannot comprehend the meaning. Without comprehending the meaning we cannot engage in meditation. Without engaging in meditation we cannot achieve realizations. This is why we need to cultivate the wisdom of listening, the wisdom of contemplation, and the wisdom of meditation.

The Foundation of All Good Qualities by Lama Tsongkhapa is a short text with a vast meaning. It is part of the genre of Buddhist teachings called the *lam-rim*—or graduated stages of the path. This text lays out the stages of the entire Buddhist path in a concise form, and presents how an individual should practice in terms of both Sutra and Tantra. For a Mahayana practitioner, knowledge of both Sutra and Tantra is extremely important because to become a fully enlightened buddha, one must have a connection to the tantric path acquired through initiation. A prerequisite for tantric initiation is the motivation of bodhicitta (the altruistic mind of enlightenment) and an understanding of emptiness. This book gives an explanation of these aspects as well as an overview of the path to complete enlightenment or buddhahood. We are also going to examine some areas that are not specifically mentioned in this lam-rim text, but which are included in more expanded versions.

We should study this teaching of the holy dharma with the purpose of achieving the most incomparable state of complete enlightenment for the benefit of all mother sentient beings.

FOUR INTRODUCTORY POINTS

For those of us who are going to include this in our practice there are four introductory points.

1. To trace the teaching to a qualified source and to authenticate them through speaking about the greatness of the author. This is the most important point.
2. The greatness and benefit of the teaching.
3. How we conduct ourselves during the discourse; in other words, how the teaching should be imparted and how the students should listen to it.
4. How an individual takes the teaching into the spiritual path.

1. Tracing the Teaching to a Qualified Source

If possible, the teaching should be able to be traced back to Shakyamuni Buddha, and to have been passed on from master to master in an unbroken chain. We have to begin with the life of the great sacred Buddha, and then follow all the lineage groups up to your present root guru, examining their practice and how they gained realizations. Lama Tsongkhapa, the author of the root verses we are studying, discusses the life of Atisha in great length in his major and middle lamrim texts, because it was Atisha who brought the integrated path of method and wisdom to Tibet.[1]

---

[1] There are two types of dharma practice: method (the extensive path) and wisdom (the profound path). Atisha integrated these two and presented them as a single path.

2. Understanding the Greatness and Benefit of the Teaching

It is essential for us to understand the greatness of the teachings so that we develop a deeper respect for them. The dharma is the most indispensable thing in our life but we need to really understand why this is so. Regardless of whether we are a beginner or whether we have been practitioners for a long time, it's very important that we understand why we need to engage in dharma practice.

The dharma can be described in two ways: scriptural (through the transmission of teachings) and also in terms of spiritual realizations. There is a sutra that says that you relieve sentient beings of their sufferings through sounding the drum of the dharma. We must thoroughly understand that if we want to find relief from our misery and predicaments and experience true happiness, the practice of the noble path of dharma is the only way.

What we hope for in our lives is for everything to be comfortable, happy, perfect and good. We don't want to experience suffering and misery or any kind of predicament, great or small. So, the two reasons why we should pursue dharma practice is to rid ourselves from misery and to find happiness.

For our practice to bear quality fruit we need to pursue it in a pure and authentic way. The greatness and effectiveness of the teachings is all there, but how much benefit we receive out of our practice depends upon the individual practitioner. How much we're willing to invest in our practice will determine the result that we gain.

3. How a Teaching Should be Conducted

This point covers the qualities one must have to be a suitable listener of the teaching, as well as what kind of qualities one must possess to dispense the teaching.

When it comes to the qualifications of the guru and disciple, there are a great many variations depending upon whether you are discussing the Vinaya (texts relating to the monastic code of ethics) Prajnaparamita (texts dealing with emptiness), or Tantrayana (the vehicle of Tantra). These variations are based on different scopes of practice. The lam-rim texts discuss the qualifications of guru and disciple in terms of the common Mahayana codes of the Bodhisattva Vehicle.

The lam-rim texts state that as a listener to the teachings, we need to learn how to rid ourselves of what are called the "three faults of a vessel". In this analogy, we are the vessel and the teaching is what is being poured into the vessel.

THE THREE FAULTS OF A VESSEL

Being Like an Upturned Vessel
1. If the vessel is turned upside down, nothing can be poured into it. In the same way, we cannot receive the teachings if our mind is distracted and we are not listening with our full attention.

Being Like a Dirty Vessel
2. If the vessel is dirty, then anything poured into it will become contaminated. This relates to a person who listens to the teachings with an impure motivation; in other words, with a worldly motivation. For example, someone who seeks to gain status and respect through their knowledge of the dharma.

Being Like a Leaky Vessel
3. If the vessel has a hole in the bottom, it will not hold any liquid. This relates to someone who hears the teachings but who doesn't retain anything afterwards.

For those of you who are new to the dharma, it may be difficult for you to grasp everything right away, but this shouldn't lead you to drop the practice. Just like learning any new skill, it's never easy in the beginning. There are always challenges. As you continue to make an effort it always gets easier, and so it will be in this case. You are not going to remain a beginner forever. When I was a freshman at the monastery and I looked at my seniors who were highly evolved, I thought, "How can I possibly ever reach that state?" Then, of course, you get there eventually. The great Acharya[2] Shantideva has said in his *Guide to the Bodhisattva's Way of Life* that however difficult something might appear, it will become easier through persistence combined with enthusiasm and effort.

When it comes to the qualifications of the teacher or guru, the lamrim talks about ten qualities. These are listed in a text called *The Ornament of Sutra (Sutralamkara)*.

THE TEN QUALITIES OF A TEACHER

A teacher should be someone who is:

1. Calm
2. Pacified
3. Totally pacified
4. Exceeding in qualification
5. Diligent
6. Has knowledge of scriptures
7. Has realized emptiness
8. Is a skilled speaker
9. Has great love for the students
10. Is not easily discouraged

1. Calm refers to someone who has the higher training of morality.
2. Pacified relates to the teacher possessing the higher training of concentration or *samadhi*.

[2] Literally, "master." An honorific title denoting someone with great spiritual and/or academic achievement.

3. Totally pacified relates to the teacher possessing the higher training of wisdom.
4. Exceeding in qualification means that the teacher must be more qualified than the students.
5. The teacher should be someone who is diligent and not inclined towards laziness.
6. The teacher should be endowed with scriptural or transmitted knowledge as a result of their studies and contemplations. If possible, this should be a person who has great authority.
7. The teacher should not only have a complete understanding of emptiness or wisdom, but if possible, should have direct realization of emptiness.
8. A teacher should be an eloquent speaker because even though they may be rich in knowledge, it will be a drawback if they lack skill in public speaking. There's a story that illustrates this.

In ancient India, there was a *mahasidda*[3] called Langkopa, who lived inside the dried carcass of an elephant. The king of the region invited Langkopa to court to give him a teaching on the ultimate reality of emptiness. Langkopa began his teaching by pointing to objects around the room, saying, "This does not exist, that does not exist," and so on. The king thought that Langkopa meant that nothing existed at all, which was clearly not the case, and concluded that the mahasidda was a misleading guide. The king was very angry and severely punished the mahasidda for giving such erroneous teachings.

Later, another mahasidda came to the palace. This teacher prepared the king for teachings on emptiness by beginning with an explanation of renunciation. He then took the king step by step through the taking of refuge, impermanence, and bodhicitta. Only then did he teach on the ultimate wisdom of emptiness. The king, who was a highly intelligent man, followed

---

[3] A highly accomplished yogi or yogini.

everything that the mahasidda taught, and gained a direct perception of emptiness. The king understood that no phenomena is self-existent and that everything exists dependently, and with this perception, all things appeared to him like an illusion. At last, he understood what Langkopa had been trying to tell him, and he deeply regretted having punished him. The point of this story is that when giving teachings to others, the method is very important.

9. The teacher should feel great love for his or her students.
10. A teacher should not become easily discouraged. For example, a teacher may find a student whom they find difficult to teach and who has trouble understanding what is being taught. Even under such challenging circumstances, the teacher should be patient and not lose hope.

THE SIX ATTITUDES OF A STUDENT

Whenever we engage in a dharma discourse we should strive to maintain the following six attitudes.

1. To view ourselves as a critically ill person.
2. To view the teaching that is being offered to us as treatment for our illness.
3. To view the teacher as a skilled doctor.
4. To understand that if we practice the dharma diligently it will cure our illness, but that we will need to seek this treatment for a great length of time in order to make a full recovery.
5. To view the Buddha as a holy being.
6. To wish for the teachings to endure in the world for a long time.

Our condition of afflictive emotions is far more serious and more damaging than any ordinary disease. There are some devastating illnesses in this world at the present time. Some are so serious that they can take your life, but this is the extent of the damage they can do. It's highly unlikely that the same illness is going to return to affect us in our next life, but when it comes to the illness of our delusions, it not only infects this present life, it also infects our future lives. Our delusions are fatal to our opportunity for happiness and cause all kinds of undesirable events to occur. All the sufferings that we experience, both major and minor, are symptoms of the delusional illness from which we suffer.

If we fall seriously ill then we need a skilled doctor, but even with a skilled doctor, if we don't follow the treatment that is prescribed, our condition will not improve. In the same way, to overcome the disease of delusions, the treatment is the holy dharma. If we want to get well, we need to not only listen to the dharma but to engage in dharma practice in its entirety.

We can find the evidence for this if we examine the lives of holy beings like the Buddha and the vast numbers of bodhisattvas who have gained total freedom from suffering and delusions. Of course, in the beginning, they were in a similar situation to ourselves, but in seeking the treatment of the dharma they reached high levels of realizations, and were eventually cured from the illness of their delusions.

This is why we should always hold the dharma in very high esteem like a sick person regards the medicine that treats their illness as their salvation. As a sick person takes refuge in their medications, so we need to learn to value the dharma. And we need to rely on a highly skilled physician-like teacher to lead us on the path. The source of the dharma is the tathagatas[4], and this is why we regard the buddhas as holy beings because it is from the buddhas that the dharma has originated.

Regarding the sixth point, at the conclusion of whatever dharma practice you do, major or minor, never forget to dedicate the merit for the longevity of the teaching.

---

[4] A Sanskrit term of veneration applied to buddhas.

4. How an Individual Takes the Teaching into the Spiritual Path

In reference to the fourth introductory point, we have to talk about the actual quintessential instructions of dharma practice and how they can lead an individual student on the spiritual path. This is where *The Foundation of All Good Qualities* begins. As you'll discover, although this text is extremely concise it is vast in the meaning it contains.

The Foundation of All Good Qualities:

THE COMMENTARY

Verse 1

1. *The foundation of all good qualities is the kind guru.*
   Cultivating the guru properly is the root of the path.
   Realizing this clearly, with great diligence,
   bless me to rely on the guru with highest devotion.

THE FIRST VERSE BEGINS *The foundation of all good qualities is the kind guru.* This refers to the guru with the ten qualifications. The guru is the source of all the teachings we receive and is the one who reveals to us the error-free path to enlightenment. Any and all realizations we gain come about through our reliance upon such a guru.

The word "foundation" in the first line is very significant. It's an all-encompassing word. Here, we can think about the grass, the trees, the rocks, the ground; the entire inheritance of the earth upon which we depend as our foundation for life. Likewise, the guru who reveals the error-free path is comparable to the earth in that he or she is the foundation of all good qualities. The guru is described as 'kind' because it is the guru who shows us the path of liberation. Therefore, the kindness of the guru is something far beyond the everyday kindness of ordinary people.

The next line reads: *Cultivating the guru properly is the root of the path.* We must cultivate our relationship with our guru in a proper manner. When you go into the lam-rim text, you'll discover that it goes into great depth about the eight great benefits of cultivating proper reliance on a guru, and the eight losses we suffer if we fail to properly cultivate our relationship with a guru, or if there's a breach in the relationship. If you understand the benefits of cultivating this proper reliance, then the quality of your relationship with your guru will be enhanced.

If we are unable to analyze this deeply, we should at least pay attention to the first line and come to appreciate that any and all positive qualities in our life stem from the guru because it is the guru who shows us the correct and unmistaken path to enlightenment.

The Tibetan master, Marpa the Translator, made three trips to India to receive teachings from his guru, Naropa—a highly accomplished siddha. Naropa bestowed on Marpa the tantric initiations and teachings of the deity Hevajra, which was Naropa's key practice.

Early one morning, Naropa summoned Marpa to his side. When Marpa arrived, he saw the entire mandala[5] of Hevajra above his guru's head, complete with the celestial palace and all the deities.

Naropa asked Marpa, "To whom are you going to prostrate first, myself or the deity Hevajra?" Marpa thought to himself, "I can see my guru any time and make prostrations to him, but I may only get this one chance to prostrate to the deity." So, Marpa answered, "I would like to prostrate to the mandala." Naropa replied. "That was a mistake. Before the guru there was no such thing as a buddha. All the buddhas of the thousand eons are the result of the guru. This meditation deity is also an emanation of the guru." With these words, Naropa snapped his fingers and dissolved the entire mandala into himself.

Once a bond between our guru and ourselves is created, it's extremely important that we make no mistake in developing that relationship. First and foremost, we should be sure to always hold the guru in high esteem and to maintain all our samaya vows[6].

---

[5] The abode of a meditational deity as the emanation of that deity.

[6] A sacred pledge taken by a practitioner that is a prerequisite for the practice of Tantra.

The words *cultivating the guru properly* can be understood as meaning both mentally and physically. This means cultivating a proper reliance on the guru through both thought and action. Of these two, however, cultivating a proper relationship with our guru through thought is more important.

Lama Tsongkhapa says that we cultivate a proper reliance on our guru through thought primarily by developing faith or respect. We do this by learning to treat our guru as more important than ourselves. One of Atisha's many disciples once asked him the following question. "In India there are a large number of people who gain very high realizations through their dharma practice, but such practitioners are rare in Tibet. Why is this?" Atisha responded, "It is because you Tibetans regard gurus just like any ordinary person." This is why we should always seek to increase and intensify our faith and respect for our gurus. In reality, gurus are emanations of buddhas, but at the very least we should learn to treat our gurus as being more important than ourselves.

The guru should be visualized as the embodiment of the entire refuge field. When Naropa meditated he had visions of the deities Tara and Avalokiteshvara. But he said, "Tara, you can be as green as you want, and Avalokiteshvara, you can be as white as you wish, but I am never separated from the aspirations of my guru." We also need to learn to treat all gurus equally. We have a tendency to offer greater respect to those gurus who sit on high thrones than to the ones with whom we live and dine.

Later, someone again asked Atisha, "In India there are many people who meditate on deities and accomplish this state, but such numbers in Tibet are very few. Why is this?" Atisha answered, "We Indians seek one deity and accomplish a hundred. You Tibetans go after a hundred deities and accomplish none." I think that this point is extremely relevant to all of us today because we like to think that such-and-such a deity is more powerful or more effective than another. We jump from one deity to the next. We start and stop, start and stop, and in the end we end up with nothing accomplished at all.

Therefore, our approach should be that of generating faith in and respect for our gurus. All our teachers of the past as well as His Holiness the Dalai Lama tell us that it is easy to maintain our respect for gurus who are often seated on high thrones, but we should be very careful to maintain our respect for those gurus with whom we interact on a daily basis. In the monastery, we monks share many teachers, so it is an area where we always have to remain particularly cautious.

Therefore, the first line of the first verse is telling us that cultivating a guru suitably becomes the root or the foundation of the path. *Realizing this clearly, with great diligence* means that when we genuinely understand this fact, we diligently work towards developing a mind of greater respect towards our gurus. We avoid insulting them at all costs, and learn to regard them not only as a person but also as a buddha. If we can learn to look upon gurus as buddhas then our reward is that we receive the blessings of the real Buddha. So, in the last line, *bless me to rely on the guru with highest devotion*, we are asking for inspiration to view our gurus with this kind of respect.

Maybe you think that you can simply study dharma books and that you don't need teachings. But we always need to have a teacher to consult with about our studies. Remember, if we wish to make an offering to our guru, no offering is greater than that of our dharma practice. Just as Milarepa said to his guru, "I have no material things to offer. I repay the kindness of my guru with my practice."

Verse 2

2. *Only once won this glorious birth of freedom.*
   By appreciating its rarity and meaningfulness
   with a mind that seizes its essence day and night,
   bless me to generate this thought continuously without cease.

The first line tells us that the kind of human life we have now is very rare. The lam-rim goes into a detailed description of how difficult it is to obtain such a birth, as well as how meaningful yet transient it is. In the context of this precious human rebirth we find discussion of the eight freedoms and ten endowments.[7] It is said that the duration of a human birth with these freedoms and endowments (sometimes referred to as leisures and riches) can be compared to the duration of a flash of lightening in a dark night. We must not waste this noble birth by using it in a meaningless way.

Not every human birth qualifies as one with freedoms and endowments. Even within the same family, not every member will necessarily have this excellent birth. If we lack the opportunity to pursue our dharma practice, for instance, then although we may have a human birth, we certainly do not have a complete human birth of freedom and endowments.

We may wonder about the words *Only once won* and think, "The number of rebirths is infinite. Of course I can get more human births in the future." But again, not every human birth qualifies as a human birth with freedoms and endowments. If we are born in an era when the teachings of Buddha and the Sangha are unavailable, then we don't have this kind of human birth.

In our own case, however, we can see that we possess these freedoms and endowments fully. We don't really have any significant external interferences or internal obstacles that prevent us from pur-

---

[7] *The eight freedoms.* Freedom from being born: with wrong views; as an animal; in a hell realm; as a hungry ghost; in a time when Buddha's teachings are unavailable; in an area too remote to gain access to the dharma or as a barbarian; mentally limited or mute; as a god.

The ten endowments. Being born a human; being born in a place with access to the dharma; having all one's organs; not being perverted by the heinous crimes; having enduring faith; being born in a time when a Buddha has come and taught the dharma; being born in a time when the teachings remain; being born in a time when the teachings are being followed; having a birth where people are generally kind and patronize the teachings.

suing the teachings and practice of the Buddha. Such an opportunity is extremely precious and immensely valuable. This is the moment in which we need to engage in perfect practice of the dharma.

There's an analogy that's used to demonstrate the rarity of this precious human rebirth. Imagine a giant turtle swimming around in a bottomless ocean. On the surface is floating a wooden yoke with a hole in its center, being carried by the currents and winds. The turtle only surfaces once every one hundred years. What are the odds that when he surfaces, the turtle will enter through the hole in the yoke? This is comparable to the chances of gaining such a perfect human birth.

What are the necessary causes that lead us to this perfect human birth? The primary cause is the observance of perfect morality. This foundation of proper ethical living is then supplemented by the practice of the six perfections (Skt: *paramitas*): generosity, ethics, patience, joyful effort, concentration, and wisdom. In addition, we should be motivated by a pure aspiration. These are the essential ingredients to achieve a human rebirth with freedoms and endowments.

The text says *By appreciating its rarity and meaningfulness*. In other words, we need to make this opportunity a meaningful one. Lama Tsongkhapa describes, *a mind that seizes its essence day and night*. He is advising us to generate the kind of mind that resolves to seek the essence from this precious human birth at all times. Just as he is requesting the inspiration or blessing to think in this way, this is what we should seek for ourselves.

THE THREE ESSENCES OF LIFE

There are three essences that we can accomplish from this precious human life. At the minimum, we can guarantee that we will not fall into the lower realms in the rebirth immediately following this life. To guarantee ourselves at least that much and working towards that is to obtain the minimum essence from our life.

The medium essence we can extract from this life is to ensure that we no longer have to dwell in cyclic existence (Skt: *samsara*). We can find freedom from cyclic existence and in doing so achieve the state of nirvana, the liberated state beyond suffering. This means that we will no longer be at the mercy of the ups and downs of cyclic existence. We can sever the continuity of cyclic existence and discontinue the repetitive round of suffering births and rebirths.

The highest essence is overcoming all the fears of the two forms of obscurations[8], and aiming for the highest enlightenment for the sake of others. This is the most perfect goal or essence that we can seek from this life.

How do we seize these essences or opportunities? We can't hire assistants to help us or negotiate, or barter to achieve them. We can only gain these essences through our own personal effort invested in pure dharma practice. If we can do this then we have made this human birth with its eight freedoms and ten endowments worthwhile. The kind of dharma that we need to pursue is the three higher trainings: higher trainings in ethics, concentration and wisdom, as well as the study of the three baskets (Skt: *tripitikas*) that contain the subject matter of these higher trainings.

We should never aim for the highest practice first, but should always try to start from the beginning. We should start with our practice of refuge and work from there in a gradual progression. If we're hurried and rushed, then the chances are that our practice will be incomplete.

We can say that we have entered the dharma path the moment that we become actively aware of the instructions with regard to which actions to avoid and which to adopt. When we are actively refraining from the actions of body, speech, and mind to be avoided and pursu-

---

[8] Obscuration to liberation (through purifying delusions) and obscuration to the omniscient state (through the development of bodhicitta—the altruistic mind of enlightenment).

ing those actions to be adopted, then our dharma practice has truly begun.

Speaking about the dharma and engaging in the dharma are not the same, just as there is a difference between having knowledge about the dharma and practicing the dharma. There are intellectuals who know a lot about dharma but who are not necessarily *in* the dharma. However, we should understand that if we want to be actively engaged in dharma practice, it's essential for us to possess intellectual knowledge.

Also, our dharma practice should not be motivated towards this present lifetime. When someone asked the great Kadam teacher Dromtönpa, "What is dharma practice?" he replied, "Give up on this life." This means that our dharma practice should never be directed towards this life's mundane and worldly concerns.

Of the three types of essence that we have discussed—preventing lower birth in our next life, attaining nirvana, and attaining complete enlightenment for the sake of others—which should we seek? If our aim is to seize the essence of complete enlightenment, then the two key ingredients are bodhicitta and the realization of emptiness.

If achieving the essence of nirvana is our goal then we must generate renunciation of cyclic existence and realization into emptiness. If we wish to prevent rebirth in a lower realm then we need to take proper refuge in the Three Jewels.

When we take refuge, we shouldn't just repeat the words mindlessly; it must be done with sincerity. When we take refuge properly two key motivating factors are present; fear of the sufferings of cyclic existence and of the lower realms in particular, and faith that the Three Jewels possess the power to provide shelter from these sufferings. If we don't have proper refuge in our mindstream then we are not yet Buddhists. We may look authentic, wearing beautiful robes and appearing very dignified, but if we do not have refuge then we cannot call ourselves a Buddhist.

This is why the ability to remain aware of the sufferings of cyclic existence, and especially of the sufferings of the lower realms, is so essential. But this is a subject that we abhor. We don't like to think about the terrible sufferings experienced by the hell beings, the hungry ghosts, and the animals.

If we dislike thinking about these things then how can we understand these sufferings on a personal level? And if we can't understand these sufferings on a personal level, then how can we generate fear for such suffering? And if we can't generate fear for such suffering, then how can we generate the motivation to avoid it? Such fear can only be generated through the proper thinking about karma and suffering. If we refuse to think about these then a major ingredient for refuge is missing.

If we have greater understanding of the abodes of the lower realms and how terrifying these places are along with the intensity of suffering that exists there, we'll do our best to personally ensure that we will never be born in such a place.

Verse 3

DEATH AND IMPERMANENCE

3. *The motion of body and life force is like a bubble, swiftly perishing.*
   Therefore, contemplate impermanence,
   for after this life, just as shadow follows form,
   good and bad karmic fruits pursue us.

How do you feel when you read this verse? Our body and life force are extremely fragile and unstable. The author compares it to a bubble on water. When you watch bubbles on water, you see how one bubble quickly arises and the next suddenly disappears. This verse is showing us how to reflect on the impermanence of personal mortality.

I'd like to remind you that all these points are for us to meditate upon so we can reinforce our studies. Through our meditation we try to make the subject matter come alive in our mindstream and to hold onto any realization we may gain from this with the help of mindfulness.

When it comes to meditating upon death and impermanence there are three major points upon which to reflect:

1. Our death is certain.
2. The time of our death is uncertain.
3. At the time of our death nothing will help except our dharma practice.

These points are greatly elaborated on in the lam-rim, but I will briefly touch upon them here.

The Certainty of Our Death

It's hard for us to really think about the certainty of our death. It's a subject that we have great difficulty comprehending. We all know that one day we're going to pass away, but that's about the extent of our understanding. We have a hard time really grasping this reality.

The lam-rim says that the changes we observe during the passing of the four seasons is one of the greatest teachers of impermanence. Just like changes take place on the outside, changes are continuously happening within our own lifespan. When we look back on our lives and our journey from birth to the present, we see how we have developed from an infant, to a child, to a youth, and so on. This progression is dramatically revealed when we look through our family photographs. When we think in this way, we can get a keener sense of the certainty of our death.

What we gain from this form of meditation is that we become inspired to minimize our indulgence in negative deeds. The reason why we engage in negative deeds is that we have a strong sense of our own permanence. This illusion of permanence leads us to act as if we are going to live forever, and to entertain harmful intent, jealousy, competitiveness, anger, etc.

If we really contemplate this subject then the quality of our dharma practice will improve. We will also experience greater harmony within our family, our friendships will intensify, and our sense of neighborhood, community, and of helping one another will all improve tremendously.

The Uncertainty of the Time of Our Death

It's actually far more important to reflect on the uncertainty of the time of our death than on the fact of our death. We all know that one day we're going to die, but we can't know when. Will it happen today? We're all confident that it won't, aren't we? The sense of the immediacy of our death is absent.

We often hear in the news how someone went to bed and was found dead the next morning, or how someone died while eating dinner or walking. We tend to think that these things only happen to other people. We need to correct this thinking and reflect that these things can very easily happen to us as well. We need to think in this way so that we work to reduce our involvement in negativities and create more virtue by engaging in meritorious activities.

We should reflect on the uncertainty of the time of our death in the following way. When we go to bed we are in human form, but we should ask ourselves "Will I still be human in the morning?" While we are eating breakfast in the morning we should ask, "Will I be alive by lunchtime?" or "I have embarked on this project, but will I die before I'm able to complete it?" It's actually very uncertain whether or not we will still be around. You can use these examples as a basis upon which to add your own experiences. If we reflect on these things very intensely then we'll find that our negative emotions are markedly reduced and begin to disappear.

Whatever topic you are meditating upon, you can use your daily activities to enhance your understanding of that area. For example, whether you're sleeping, lying down, or up and walking around, all your activities can be used to further your understanding of impermanence. If you are focusing on other topics such as precious human rebirth or cultivating the guru, again you can involve those thoughts in all your activities.

At the Time of Our Death Nothing Will Help Except the Dharma

When death comes there is no difference between a king and a pauper. For a king surrounded by his royal wealth and a pauper in poverty and destitution, death is the same.

When we die, neither the wealth and material things we've accumulated, nor the friendships and relationships we've cultivated will be of any value. None of our loved ones can keep us company. We make our journey into death all alone. Our only hope is whatever virtuous actions we have accumulated because our karma is the only thing that can accompany us into the next life. Nothing else.

Our friends, loved ones, and dear relatives to whom we feel so close that it's almost palpable; any one of them would gladly keep you company on your journey into death if they could. In ancient Egypt, the Pharaohs were buried together with their queens because it was assumed that they would make the journey through death together. But even if you're buried in the same spot as another person or someone dies at exactly the same time as you, each person must make the journey into the next life separately. Just as we are born alone, so is our journey at death.

We come to the conclusion that at the moment of death nothing is of any value except the dharma. These thoughts will become one of the greatest motivators for our practice. If we're able to engage in sound dharma practice, then this will remain with us forever. Dharma practice is intangible. It isn't something you can hold in your hand. It can only reside in your mind. In the same way, when we accumulate a negative deed that also resides in our mind.

Although the negative deeds and afflictive emotions that we've gathered reside in our mind, they're not blended *with* our mind. That's why Maitreya Buddha[9] said that all the stains upon our mind are temporary and adventitious. What he meant by this is that all the negative deeds and delusions contaminating our mind can be successfully cleansed. Afflictive emotions cling to the mind like dirt clings to cloth. Just as we can remove the dirt from our clothes, we can reach a point where we can separate the stains of afflictive emotions and the mind from each other. When we remove the dirt from our clothes, this doesn't destroy the cloth because the cloth and the dirt are not one and the same. Likewise, negativities and the mind are not the same. When we remove negativities from the mind, the mind is not destroyed.

As the Buddha said, the real nature of the mind is luminous and radiant, meaning that we have buddha nature or buddha potential within our mindstream. This isn't some vague assumption. We can prove the existence of buddha nature with the lowest form of logic and reasoning.

The lam-rim says that among all meditations, the one that is the most effective and profound is the meditation on impermanence and death. This is because if we can remain constantly aware of death and impermanence then we can engage in dharma spontaneously, and whatever dharma we pursue will be of high quality. Meditation on death and impermanence will also inspire us to stay the course—to pursue the path to completion. As it says in the first line of verse three, our life is *swiftly perishing*, so we should constantly remain aware of death.

The author goes on to say that just like shadow follows form, good and bad karmas follow us into death.[10] After death, the results of what-

---

[9] The name of the next buddha to appear in our world.

[10] In this text, the subject of karma comes after discussion of death and impermanence, whereas in other lam-rim texts the taking of refuge is presented after death and impermanence.

ever good and bad karmas you have accumulated will keep you company into the next life.

THE FOUR POINTS OF KARMA

The Buddha taught that there are four laws of karma: 1/ once a karma is created its fruition is certain; 2/ karma that is not purified multiplies in power; 3/ we do not encounter the fruit of karma for which we're not responsible; and 4/ karma never goes away of its own accord.

It's very important to become acquainted with these facts of karma. Regarding the first point, if we've created the karma to be born in any of the six realms of migratory beings, for example, we will follow that karma to that destination.

The second point is karma's multiplying power. However minor our karma might appear to us, virtuous or non-virtuous, it multiplies exponentially. If we create a karma one today, that karma multiplies by two tomorrow, four by the next day, eight by the following day, and so on. This applies equally to both virtuous and non-virtuous deeds. If you kill an ant today, it is like you killed two ants by tomorrow, four the next day and eight the following day. Likewise, if you save the life of an ant today, that will become like saving two ants tomorrow, and so on. If you said the mantra *om mani padme hum* one time today, the same act doubles tomorrow, quadruples the next day, and on and on.

The third point is that we will not encounter the maturation of karma for which we're not responsible. We are responsible for any karma that matures in our lives, and no one else's karma is going to bear its fruit upon us. John's good or bad karma will never come to fruition on Peter, for example. If you have not perpetrated a karma, you will never face the maturation or the fruit of that karma. In the 2004 tsunami in Thailand, an entire train was washed away and almost all the passengers died. There was a story about one small child who climbed a tree and managed to survive against all odds. Why was this child spared when everyone else was killed? This is because the child had not created the karma to be killed in that way at that time.

During the time of the Buddha there was a great battle between an Indian kingdom ruled by King Salgyal and the clan of the Shakyas. King Salgyal's troops got the upper hand in the fight and many Shakyas were killed. Buddha's attendant, Ananda, pleaded with the Buddha, "You teach that all sentient beings are like our mothers, and here are the Shakyas being massacred. Please grant protection to them."

The Buddha understood that this battle was the fruition of past karma and that it would not be of much use to intervene. But to comply with Ananda's request he used his supernatural power to bring two young Shakyas from the battlefield and placed them next to him. When the battle was over, however, the two young men whom the Buddha had rescued from the battlefield were dead along with all the other Shakya soldiers. No one had attacked them, they were far away from the fighting, but their karma was such that they had also perished. If the maturation of a karma is in progress, it cannot be altered, even by a buddha.

For example, there are many different causes of insanity: intense fear, a chemical imbalance, an imbalance in the body's elements, deep sorrow, intense greed, and so on. Some become mentally ill simply because of the natural progression of their karma. In this latter case, no ordinary treatment can help. If mental or physical illness is brought about from the maturation of a karma, then I think the best treatment is the collection of merit and the purification of negativities.

There are ten virtuous actions and ten non-virtuous actions. As we come to an understanding that all these deeds in which we engage are following us everywhere we go, we try to ensure that we never engage in non-virtue and try to practice as much virtue as we can. As it says in this verse, *for after this life, just as shadow follows form, good and bad karmic fruits pursue us.*

Verse 4

4. *With this firm conviction,*
   abandoning even the smallest non-virtue
   and engaging in every virtuous deed,
   bless me to always live conscientiously.

Verse 5

5. *Samsaric splendors are never satisfying,*
   they are unreliable and the door to all misery.
   Seeing these faults, for the joy of Nirvana,
   bless me to generate intense enthusiasm.

THE SIX FAULTS OF SAMSARA

All three worlds and all the realms of cyclic existence are *unreliable* or undependable. There are six main flaws or faults of samsara or cyclic existence. Samsara is described as flawed because it:

1. is not dependable
2. is never satisfying
3. requires us to repeatedly discard our physical form
4. requires us to repeatedly enter conception and birth in the six realms
5. causes us to continually fluctuate in status
6. makes us isolated from one another

1. The Fault of Not Being Dependable

Of the six realms of cyclic existence there isn't one that we can single out and say with confidence "I have never taken birth in that place." We have been circling through samsara in every one of those realms. We've had multiple births as devas or gods, where we've enjoyed beautiful environments, great friends, wealth, and pleasure. We've taken birth in such places not just once but countless times. But since uncertainty is one of the features of cyclic existence, we have also fallen from those abodes countless times.

We've also been countless times in the lowest state of the hells. The fact that at present we're all human, again shows the unreliability of cyclic existence. Even though we've been born in a hell realm, the maturation of the karmas that got us there eventually came to an end.

The Tibetan drawing of cyclic existence is called *sidpa khorlo* or the wheel of life. *Sidpa* is samsara and *khorlo* is circle, and in this drawing we see depictions of the six realms. It's within these six realms that we're circling or cycling. When we achieve liberation (Skt: *moksha*) we break free from that cycle and attain nirvana, the state beyond suffering.

We wander about in samsara compelled by karma and delusions. So, as Arya Nagarjuna states in his *Fundamental Wisdom Treatise (Mulamadhyamika Karika)* when karma and delusions are exhausted, that's liberation. Arya Nagarjuna eloquently states that nirvana or liberation is not something far off in the distance; it is right here. When we manage to bring karma and delusions to total exhaustion within our human form, we have become *arhats* and have achieved liberation. In India and Tibet there are many examples of mahasiddhas—highly accomplished beings who have attained liberation. They didn't go very far at all in terms of distance; liberation was within them.

2. The Fault of Never Satisfying

Cyclic existence is never fulfilling. In Tibetan the description literally translates to "unquenchable". Through our desire we indulge in *samsaric splendors* or pleasures, but we are never satisfied with the happiness we receive from them. We are just like a thirsty person drinking salt water. The more we drink, the more our thirst increases. In the same way, the more we indulge in samsaric pleasures, the greater our discontent.

That's why Arya Nagarjuna says in his *Precious Garland (Ratnavali)* "Indulging in samsaric pleasure is like scratching an itch." The more you scratch an itch, the stronger the itch becomes, and the more you need to scratch.

What are *samsaric splendors*? They are the sensory objects of form, sound, taste, smell, and touch. The more we engage with these five sensory objects, the more we desire them. As our desire increases, we degenerate. This is why one of the most useful tools for us to develop is a sense of contentment with what we have.

3. The Fault of Making us Repeatedly Discard our Physical Form
4. The Fault of Making us Repeatedly Enter Conception and Birth in the Six Realms

As long as we choose to stay within cyclic existence, we are subjected to relinquishing our body again and again. Each time after giving up our body, we have to re-enter conception and birth.

5. The Fault of Causing us to Continually Fluctuate in Status

We experience extreme variations in the kinds of births we take, from very high births in the god realms to births in the hells. In the Seventh Dalai Lama's *Prayer to Avalokiteshvara*, he says, even a person holding the highest position of authority can soon find themselves a slave. Maybe we are a powerful ruler in this life, but because of our karma we are born as a pauper in our next. Our body is like a withering flower, and our wealth is like borrowed jewelry.

6. The Fault of Loneliness

The lam-rim speaks about the loneliness of samsara. It means that although there is a period of time when we enjoy a great number of people; our family members, friends, and colleagues; when we die we face a very final separation from them all.

We are all driven by attachment and aversion, which is why we're unable to maintain an attitude of equanimity. We're always experiencing a sense of distance from some people and an extreme closeness to a chosen few. All these feelings come about because of the desirous nature of cyclic existence. This is why when we make mandala offerings, we offer the objects of attachment, aversion, and ignorance, and we seek to offer them without any sense of loss.

THE MIND OF RENUNCIATION

When we clearly comprehend all these flaws of cyclic existence, then we will wish to make every effort towards achieving the joy of liberation. Once we are able to produce a mind of renunciation (literally "definite deliverance") then we'll be able to generate a powerful aspiration or *intense enthusiasm* for nirvana. As the fifth verse states *Seeing these faults, for the joy of Nirvana, bless me to generate intense enthusiasm.*

The first teaching that the Buddha gave on the Four Noble Truths[11] was on the truth of suffering. If we don't comprehend the truth of suffering, then our desire to break away from the source of suffering will be weak. Therefore, out of his great loving compassion, the Buddha spoke first about the truth of suffering to inspire us to seek freedom from suffering.

Lama Tsongkhapa states that if we don't make an effort to understand the flaws of cyclic existence or the truth of suffering, then we won't develop any will to break away from its source. As Maitreya Buddha states in the *Uttaratantra*, to cure an illness, a doctor needs to be able to understand the patient's symptoms and diagnose the condition. Only then can he or she prescribe the appropriate medicine that will eliminate the cause of the illness.

If you can produce a strong mind of renunciation or the mind of definite deliverance (Tib: *ngejung gi sampa*), you will become extremely interested in pursuing nirvana. And if enthusiasm for nirvana is strong, then it will take much less effort to accomplish this goal. That's why

[11] The Four Noble Truths are: the truth of suffering, the truth of the causes of suffering, the truth of the cessation of suffering, and the truth of the path that leads one out of suffering.

in Lama Tsongkhapa's text *The Three Principle Aspects of the Path*, the first principle aspect is renunciation.

Verse 6

6. *Inspired by this immaculate determination,*
   with mindfulness, alertness, and great conscientiousness,
   bless me to pursue the pratimoksha vows—the root of the teaching,
   as my core practice.

This immaculate determination refers to the mind of renunciation, which is an immaculate or pure thought. The next line says, *with mindfulness, alertness, and great conscientiousness. Mindfulness* is what enables us to maintain the object of meditation without losing it, whereas the function of *alertness* is to monitor and correct any impediments to our meditation. Then the *great conscientiousness* enables us to engage in the practice properly and conscientiously.

The pratimoksha[12] vows are described in the third line as *the root of the teaching.* There are seven sets of pratimoksha vows within which we find three classes: 1/ the layperson's (Skt: *upasaka*) vows; 2/ the vows of novice nuns and monks; and 3/ the vows of fully ordained nuns (Skt: *bhikshunis*) and fully ordained monks (Skt: *bhikshus*). All these vows are referred to as individual emancipation vows, and are regarded as the very foundation of the teaching.

The way in which we determine if a tantric teaching is viable and present is by whether or not the empowerment, the transmission, and teachings on that tantric practice are available. If they are, then we can say that the tantric teaching is present and viable.

The way we judge whether or not a sutra teaching is preserved is by the lineage of the pratimoksha vows. If the vows of novice and fully

---

[12] Pratimoksha means liberation from cyclic existence and refers to the vows given by the Buddha to his followers.

ordained nuns and monks are prevalent, including the tradition of taking, keeping, and restoring the vows, then the teachings of the Buddha are said to also be present and viable.

In other words, the way that we determine whether the teachings of Buddha continue to exist isn't by whether or not there continue to be shrines, temples, or monasteries. Instead, we need to look inward to the individual mindstream and to an individual's ethical or moral discipline. Of the three higher trainings, the first is the higher training of morality. Once we develop the higher training of morality, we can generate the higher training of concentration (Skt: *samadhi*) and thus produce the higher training of wisdom.

The last line that reads *bless me to pursue the pratimoksha vows—the root of the teaching*, also has the connotation of engaging in the practice faithfully to completion. This means not only doing our practice, but practicing meticulously and bringing that practice to its consummation.

Verse 7

7. *Just as I have fallen into the ocean of samsara*
   so too have wandering motherly beings.
   Seeing this, bless me to develop the altruistic mind
   that assumes the responsibility to free them all.

Cyclic existence is compared to an ocean because just like samsara the ocean's depths are difficult to detect. Also, if you are caught out in the ocean, it can be difficult to find your way to shore. Furthermore, just as the ocean is full of dangers such as strong currents and sharks, samsara is also a dangerous place. For these reasons, we often find reference to the *ocean of samsara*. Remember, when we speak about samsara, we're never looking outward towards a physical location. The ocean of cyclic existence is very personal. It is within us from birth and will continue with us until we break away and find liberation.

Among all the realms in cyclic existence, we humans have the best kind of birth. When we compare our lives to those of the beings in hell, the hungry ghosts, and the animals, we can easily see that this life is far better than theirs by any standard. Even so, when we look deeply at our own life, we can see how it consists of a multitude of various forms of suffering.

From our understanding of how difficult it is to be in samsara through our personal experience, we then try to reflect upon the predicament of other sentient beings with the understanding that they are in a similar situation to us.

As it says in verse seven, *Just as I have fallen into the ocean of samsara, so too have wandering motherly beings.* Others are also caught in the waves of this unbearable ocean of cyclic existence. So, we begin with a personal understanding and then develop this understanding beyond ourselves to include other beings.

There is a text which states, 'We're caught in the net of self-grasping and the darkness of ignorance is all around. We are continually oppressed by the three forms of suffering: the suffering of suffering, the suffering of change, and the suffering of conditioning. Through understanding the situation of my mothers, may I generate the supreme mind.' The root text reads *Seeing this, bless me to develop the altruistic mind that assumes the responsibility to free them all.* These two quotes are very similar. Verse seven talks about accepting the responsibility of ending the suffering of others. This means that we resolve to seek the tools and the means with which we can remove the sufferings of other sentient beings. In this search, we discover that achieving buddhahood is the only way to really help others successfully and we resolve to become a buddha to help other sentient beings end their suffering. The mind that assumes this burden is called the 'supreme mind' or *bodhicitta.*

This precious bodhicitta is of two types: wishing and engaging. Acharya Shantideva described them as the difference between planning a trip and actually traveling. Wishing bodhicitta is having the will or intention to achieve buddhahood for others. With engaging bodhicitta, you're not just *intending* to become a buddha, you're actually engaging in all the necessary practices such as the six perfections of the bodhisattvas in order to achieve buddhahood. The moment you achieve either wishing or engaging bodhicitta, then you're on the Mahayana path of accumulation and your path to buddhahood has begun.

In the last two lines of verse seven *bless me to develop the altruistic mind that assumes the responsibility to free them all,* we are praying for the inspiration to train in and generate the supreme mind of bodhicitta. Of course, simply praying for this to come about is not adequate. We need to work and cultivate the tools with which we can produce bodhicitta within our mind.

When we are trying to train in bodhicitta, it is helpful if we first meditate on the vast benefits of cultivating this kind of attitude. Acharya Shantideva has said that just as the right alchemical catalysts can transform base metals into gold, this impure body of ours can transform into the body of a buddha with the help of bodhicitta.

We have accumulated enormous stores of negativities from many lifetimes in the past that we need to purify. There's no better way to eliminate these negativities than by meditating on bodhicitta. Nothing exceeds the power of bodhicitta to purify negative karma.

The reason that bodhicitta is so effective in purifying negativities becomes clear when we consider how our negativities are committed. It is always in relation to sentient beings that we commit negativities. The aim of bodhicitta is to enable us to become a buddha so that we can help other beings to achieve buddhahood themselves. Bodhicitta is always aimed at becoming a buddha for the sake of others, never just for the sake of oneself. This is why the root of virtue created through bodhicitta is so effective. It is why Acharya Shantideva describes bodhicitta as the butter of all the Buddha's teachings. Through churning the milk of the Buddha's teachings we obtain its essence—the butter-like bodhicitta.

The moment that you develop bodhicitta, no matter what kind of being you are, you become worthy of the respect of the entire world. Maitreya's *Ornament of Clear Realization (Abhisamayalamkara)*, describes two areas where one can receive bodhicitta—the mental base and physical base. The mental base constitutes inner qualities such as faith, great compassion, and great loving-kindness. As a physical base, bodhicitta is possible to develop in any of the six realms of samsara. If it's possible for a hell being or an animal to generate bodhicitta, then it's certainly very possible for us as human beings. We should continually aspire to generate bodhicitta. We should read and repeat this prayer as much as we can; "*May the precious bodhi mind not yet born arise and grow, may that born have no decline but increase forever more.*" We should try to bring our minds ever closer to the meaning of this prayer.

METHODS FOR DEVELOPING BODHICITTA

When we're trying to train in and develop bodhicitta, there are two methods available to us. One method goes back to the great prince, Acharya Shantideva, which he inherited from Manjushri through Arya Nagarjuna. Another method is traced back to Acharya Asanga, which he inherited from Maitreya Buddha.

A tradition that comes to us through Acharya Shantideva is known as *dagshen nyamjey*. Dag means 'self' and shen means 'others'. Nyam means 'equal' and jey means 'exchange'. So *dagshen nyamjey* translates to 'equalizing and exchanging self with others'.

The tradition that comes down through Acharya Asanga is called 'the six causes and one result'. Some texts list seven causes, while others list eight. When eight causes are counted, the development of immeasurable equanimity is listed as number one. When we cultivate great equanimity we try to even out our attitude towards three kinds of people: adversaries, friends, and strangers. We share them equally as our object of meditation, and then generate an unbiased attitude towards them all. We use lines of reasoning such as the fact that our friends and adversaries were all strangers at one time. There is a Tibetan saying, 'No one starts out as an enemy, neither does anyone start out as a friend.' How many times have these roles switched in this lifetime alone? An enemy becomes a friend, a friend becomes an adversary, and so on. Just as these roles can switch rapidly in this life, so they have done in all our past lives.

What we're trying to do is eliminate our dislike for our adversaries and remove our attachment to our friends, and in doing so create an impartial attitude towards them all. When you contemplate and mediate on these topics, the realization that you will gain is that you will make no distinction between enemies, friends, and strangers. You will view all three kinds of people alike.

THE SIX CAUSES AND ONE RESULT
1. Understanding all sentient beings to be your mothers
2. Remembering the kindness of all sentient beings
3. Determining to repay their kindness
4. Wishing all sentient beings to have happiness (love)
5. Wishing all sentient beings to be free from suffering (compassion)
6. Taking the responsibility to relieve all sentient beings of their suffering

Bodhicitta (the result)

1. Understanding All Sentient Beings to be Your Mothers
When you have developed an experience of equanimity then you are ready to advance to step one: seeing all beings as your kind mothers. We do this through the application of logic and then we induce a sense of conviction through meditation. We first think of our present birth

and then of our immediate past life. We then try to think back to our former lives. Eventually, we come to a sense of the beginninglessness of the cycle of rebirths. Of course, the origins of our physical body don't go that far back, but when we think about our current mind, we sense that it is somehow connected to the mind we had earlier. There's a sense of continuity. Today's mind is connected with the mind of yesterday, and the mind of yesterday with the mind of the day before, and so on. We can trace this continuity of mind all the way to conception and to the point when we first entered our mother's womb.

Where did that first fresh consciousness at the moment of this life's conception come from? It came from the *bardo*, the in-between state prior to birth, and the mind of the bardo came from a prior life. This is how we trace the stream of consciousness.

When we discover through this kind of analysis that our birth as such has no beginning, we realize that we cannot reduce the role of mother to the claim of any single sentient being. We are brought to the conclusion that each and every one of these sentient beings has served as our mother or our other relations in the past.

We may find this difficult to accept, and think, if this is true then why don't I remember it? But think about how much we actually recall from our early infancy in this life, and here we're talking about a cycle of multiple deaths and births. When we deliberate upon this topic it's called 'meditating on the recognition of all as mothers.' When you gain experience of this, whomever you meet, you recognize that person as your kind mother.

2. Remembering the Kindness of All Sentient Beings

The second step is thinking about the kindness of our mothers. Borrowing from this life's experience, we think about how much care and concern our mothers have bestowed upon us. From this we can infer that in a previous life we have been raised with the same level of care and concern by those whom we now count as our adversaries. The kindness of the mother can be clearly seen even in the animal kingdom. A mother bird will sacrifice herself to save her chicks, for example, or a doe will do everything she can to provide for and protect her babies. The sign that we have truly realized the enormous kindness of other sentient beings is that we perceive everyone we meet as being incredibly kind.

3. Determining to Repay their Kindness

The third step is our will to repay this kindness. What is it that can be of real benefit to other sentient beings? What's the primary thing that they really need? Food, clothing, and shelter are all necessary, but they give only temporary satisfaction. None of these things can satisfy our ultimate needs. What sentient beings really want is total separation from misery and true and lasting happiness. This is a wish shared by even the smallest insect.

4. Wishing All Sentient Beings to Have Happiness (Love)

The fourth step is meditating on loving-kindness, assuming all sentient beings as the focus of our meditation. This means that we cannot exclude anyone. We can't leave someone out simply because we dislike them. Actually, we should make a point to include in this meditation those people whom we dislike and give special attention to them, wishing that they be endowed with all happiness.

This is just like when you're meditating on the second of the four immeasurables.[13] You think, "*How wonderful it would be if all sentient beings had happiness and its causes. May they have these. I shall cause them to have these. Bless me to be able to do so.*"

In your meditation on great loving-kindness (Skt: *mahamaitri*) you focus upon all sentient beings, and with as much intensity as you can

---

[13] The four immeasurables are: immeasurable equanimity, immeasurable love, immeasurable compassion, and immeasurable joy.

generate, you wish that they become endowed with happiness and the essential causes of happiness. Don't just recite these prayers or verses in a perfunctory manner. Instead, make their meaning come from the depth of your heart, free of any envy or jealousy. If you can do this then it's a cause for great joy, and this joy then further intensifies your wish for the happiness of others. If you see someone whom you dislike achieve some success and you feel envious, that's a sign that you don't have great loving-kindness. When you have great loving-kindness you want more success for others than for yourself. When this happens you are ready to advance to the next step—meditating on great compassion.

5. Wishing All Sentient Beings to be Free From Suffering (Compassion)

When you engage in meditation on great compassion (Skt: *mahakaruna*) the focal object of your meditation is again all sentient beings. The difference between great loving-kindness and great compassion is in the way they manifest. The way that loving-kindness manifests is in your aspiration that others be endowed with happiness and its causes. The way that great compassion manifests is in your wish for others to be free of suffering and its causes. This is like when you are meditating on the third of the four immeasurables. "*How wonderful it would be if all sentient beings were free of suffering and its causes. May they be free. I shall cause them to be free. Bless me to be able to do so.*" When you generate great compassion, you will not harm any being either physically or mentally. If you come across, hear about, or recall any sentient being afflicted with pain, you experience the urgent wish for their relief.

There is also a difference between great compassion and immeasurable compassion. Great compassion shares all sentient beings as the object of meditation, whereas immeasurable compassion, though it shares immeasurable sentient beings as its object of meditation, does not assume *all* sentient beings as its object of meditation. For example, in the city of Los Angeles, the number of beings are immeasurable but there are many other beings in many other realms of existence. Only when you include *all* sentient beings as the object of meditation can you generate great compassion. The same thing goes for immeasurable loving-kindness and great loving-kindness.

It is said that pratyekabuddhas (*solitary realizers*) and shravakas (*hearers*) do not have great compassion. When you have great compassion, you no longer abide in the extreme of solitary peace (*nirvana*) because you aspire to help other sentient beings to become free from their suffering. As Maitreya says in *Abhisamayalamkara*, "Who has great compassion will not fall down into solitary peace."

We can assume that we have gained a certain degree of experiential realization of great compassion if upon seeing, hearing about, or recalling any sentient being afflicted with suffering, we spontaneously feel as if this suffering is happening to our own child or best friend, and we feel a strong desire for them to be free of that suffering.

6. Taking the Responsibility to Relieve All Sentient Beings of their Suffering

The sixth point is called *lhagsam* in Tibetan. *Lhag* means 'exceptional' and *sam* means 'thought', so *lhagsam* means 'exceptional thought' or 'exceptional intention'. You have meditated on great compassion and generated the strong wish for all sentient beings to be free from suffering, and yet you still haven't assumed that responsibility yourself. The exceptional thought is when you feel, "I shall personally assume responsibility to free all sentient beings of suffering." However, you realize that at present you don't have the ability to do this and that only a buddha can free all beings from suffering. You then determine to become a buddha to be able to achieve this goal.

Bodhicitta (The Result)

When we have seen this meditation through to its completion, bodhichitta is right there, totally accessible, as the mind focusing upon all sentient beings with the determination to lead them all to the state of buddhahood.

EQUALIZING AND EXCHANGING SELF FOR OTHERS

The other tradition for generating bodhicitta that comes to us via Shantideva from Acharya Nagarjuna is called 'equalizing and exchanging self for others.' In this method you deliberate upon five major points.

1. The equality of self and others
2. The flaws of self-cherishing
3. The benefits of cherishing others
4. The actual exchange of self with others
5. Tonglen meditation (giving and receiving)

1. The Equality of Self and Others

The first step is understanding that self and others are equal. No matter what kind of sentient being you are, regardless of your size or status, none of us desires even the slightest misery. We're all equal in the sense that we all desire happiness and dislike suffering.

When we come to the full realization of our equality with other sentient beings, we will stop harming them in any way; mentally, verbally, or physically, because we will understand that when we inflict any kind of harm upon others it's just like inflicting that same harm upon ourselves.

When it comes to comfort and joy, no matter how trivial, we are never contented and feel that we can never get enough. The same is true for others. So, when you see other sentient beings enjoying themselves, you'll be able to rejoice in their happiness and success and share in their delight totally free from envy or jealousy. If you plan to engage in this meditation, then you may want to write 'self and others are equal' on a piece of paper in large letters and post it wherever it's easy for you to see it.

All of these points are materials for meditation. They're not just for chatting about. It's through meditation that we make these materials personal and gain realizations that make them part of our experience.

2. The Flaws of Self-Cherishing

The second point is to deliberate on the flaws of self-cherishing from all angles. We examine how all the undesirable things we experience in our lives are the result of self-cherishing. It is because of self-cherishing that we hold ourselves more precious than others. We kill others, we steal from others, we lie, use harsh and divisive words, we gossip and engage in sexual misconduct, malevolent thoughts, covetousness, and other negative mental activities. All our problems arise from inflicting harm upon other beings, and we are motivated to do this by the attitude that cares for the self more than for others.

When we hold ourselves so dear and precious there is no end to what we want. We feel we must prevail over others, and this is the source of all war and profiteering. Panchen Lobsang Chökyi Gyaltsen compares self-cherishing to a chronic illness. But the worst thing that a chronic illness can do is to take your life, and it's more than likely that you'll return in your next life. The consequences of self-cherishing are far worse. All kinds of undesirable events come about as a result. So, we shouldn't point the finger at others and blame them for our miseries. We should point the finger directly at the guilty party— our self-cherishing attitude. We have abundant material for this meditation because every single day we go through a variety of experiences: neutral, gloomy, joyful, and so on. So, you can think about this every single day. It's through probing the flaws of self-cherishing that we begin to work towards removing it.

3. The Benefits of Cherishing Others

The third point is to try to consider all the benefits of cherishing others. We need to understand that every single good quality and experience in our lives is the result of holding others dear. As Acharya

Shantideva says, "All the happiness that exists in the world comes from wanting others to be happy. All the suffering that exists in the world comes from wanting happiness for oneself." Compelled by self-cherishing we engage in acts that are harmful to others, and it is from such acts that all our sufferings flow.

How do we know that cherishing others is the source of all happiness? All we have to do is to look at the lives of the buddhas and high level bodhisattvas who cherish others so much, and see how much happiness, ease, and comfort they experience.

In the beginning, it's easier to choose subjects that are close to you such as your immediate friends and family members. When you can successfully do this meditation in relation to them, you can then expand it to include others.

4. The Actual Exchange of Self with Others

The fourth step is the actual exchange of self with others. There's nothing physically exchanged. What is being exchanged is one's attitudes towards self and others. Previously, we've ignored others and cherished the self. But now we're trying to substitute these attitudes, so that instead we ignore self and cherish others. We're trying to displace our own personal purposes and choose the purposes of others; to become less concerned with self-interest and to place a greater priority on the interests of others.

5. The Practice of Tonglen (Giving and Receiving)

The fifth point is based on all the previous ones and is the practice of tonglen. Tonglen means 'giving and receiving.' The one who is giving and receiving is the self, and the ones to whom you send and from whom you receive are other sentient beings.

What we receive from sentient beings is whatever is undesirable for them such as an illness or mental anguish. We receive these sufferings from all other sentient beings in the form of a dark light. At the same time at the core of our heart we visualize another dark light, which represents our ignorant self-grasping and all our afflictive emotions, particularly the three poisons: ignorance, anger, and attachment. We bring the dark light we've collected from sentient beings towards us, drawing it in through our nostrils and down to our heart. The moment that these two dark lights make contact at the core of our heart, both lights immediately disperse. Don't hold onto them or let them settle in. Instead, imagine that they disappear or are destroyed, just like when you're in a dark room and the darkness disappears the moment that a bright light is switched on.

Then in the form of white light we visualize sending out through our nostrils whatever small joys, happiness, realizations, and knowledge we have, and all that we're going to achieve in the future, including all the realizations and great qualities of buddhahood. This white light travels out and merges into the sentient beings, satisfying all that they need and desire. When you engage in this practice, you intensify your compassion through receiving suffering from others, and you also intensify the strength of your loving-kindness by sending them happiness.

Verse 8

8. *If this resolve is created*
   yet habituation in the three ethics is lacking,
   enlightenment cannot be achieved.
   Realizing this fully, bless me to train in the
   bodhisattva precepts with strong enthusiasm.

After generating bodhicitta, we need to engage in the deeds of the Buddha's children—the bodhisattvas. These are the *six perfections* or *paramitas*. The practice of the six perfections is how those on the bodhisattva path involve themselves in the causes of sentient beings and simultaneously mature their own mental continuum.

As it states in the first line, *If this resolve is created* (meaning the resolve to become enlightened for the sake of others) *yet habituation in the three ethics is lacking*. Therefore, one must become familiar with and guard the three moralities: the morality of abstaining from misdeeds, the morality of involving ourselves in the welfare of others, and the morality of engaging in virtuous deeds. All the activities of the six perfections are included within these three moralities of abstention, involvement, and engagement.

The morality of abstaining from misdeeds means keeping the bodhisattva vows—the eighteen root vows and the forty-six secondary vows. In all our activities, we make sure to observe these vows properly and never to transgress any of them. For instance, if you're a monk, this means properly keeping your monastic vows. If you're a layperson, then it means keeping the bodhisattva vows, tantric vows, refuge vows, and so forth. Safeguarding every one of the vows we've taken is the morality of abstaining from misdeeds.

Being involved in the welfare of sentient beings means helping others without any bias or discrimination. Specifically, it refers to how bodhisattvas mature the mindstreams of others by engaging in the four ways of gathering disciples: practicing generosity, speaking politely and appropriately, fulfilling their needs, and acting in accordance with the teachings received. Any help that you provide to other sentient beings inspired by bodhicitta is being involved in the welfare of sentient beings.

As for the third morality—engaging in virtuous deeds—any deeds we perform motivated or inspired by bodhicitta become the morality of engaging in virtue. Therefore, for the bodhisattva, all actions: making offerings, performing prostrations, reciting prayers, etc., become actions of virtuous engagement. No action is ignored or singled out.

In Tibetan, morality (*tsultim*) is defined as 'the will to protect'. What this means is the will to protect our vows, free of any transgressions. The author emphasizes that mere knowledge of these moralities is not adequate. He uses the word *habituation* meaning that we need to become accustomed to practicing these ethical guidelines. If we fail to do so, we will not be able to attain the body of enlightenment and the incomparable state of buddhahood.

The last two lines of verse eight read, *Realizing this fully, bless me to train in the bodhisattva precepts with strong enthusiasm.* So, we're seeking inspiration to train in these precepts or deeds with a strong sense of eagerness.

We shouldn't think that these deeds: the six perfections, the four ways of gathering disciples, and the three moralities, are just for bodhisattvas. We need to apply these practices in whatever way we can at the present time. Even if we can only emulate the bodhisattvas, the time will come when we can actually perform these deeds to their level of ability.

Verse 9

9. *That which prevents distraction towards distorted objects*
   and enables analytic penetration into the perfect meaning,
   bless me to quickly produce in my mindstream
   the integrated path of shamatha and vipashyana.

The first line refers to calm abiding (Skt. *shamatha*) which prevents the mind from getting distracted by distorted objects; in other words, objects that inspire our delusions. What enables us to analytically penetrate the ultimate nature of reality or the *perfect meaning* is *vipashyana* or 'special insight.'

Lama Tsongkhapa emphasizes that these two capabilities, shamatha and vipashyana, cannot properly combat our afflictive emotions by themselves. We need to combine the two into one. This is why Lama Tsongkhapa refers to *the integrated path of shamatha and vipashyana* that produces the mind of single-pointed concentration or *samadhi.*

In Lama Tsongkhapa's *Lines of Experience*, he writes that concentration rules supreme above all mind. Once this mind is placed upon a chosen object of meditation, it remains there unwavering and unshakeable like Mount Meru[14] itself. If we then use this mind to pursue any virtuous action, we will be able to penetrate the nature of reality and gain direct realization into emptiness. Calm abiding brings about a great physical and mental agility or pliancy (Tib: *shinjang*), and an extremely workable state of both body and mind. The physical pliancy makes your body feel light like a ball of cotton wool. As a result of this some meditators can even levitate. Mental pliancy produces a state of intense bliss (Tib: *dechen*), but physical lightness and mental bliss are not the intended aims of shamatha (Tib: *shinnay*). What we're trying to achieve with shamatha is the stability to generate discriminating awareness or wisdom (Tib: *prajna*).

There is an analogy inspired by ancient warfare. Shamatha is compared to a sturdy, reliable horse. The meditator is the one who is mounted on the horse. The weapon with which the rider is going to fight the enemy is the wisdom understanding emptiness.

The saying goes, 'Mounting on the stable horse of shamatha with the sharp weapon of the view of madhyamika[15], free of all extremes, one can then sever the object of negation—the self-grasping attitude.'

Generally speaking, calm abiding meditation is not an exclusively Buddhist practice. Both Buddhists and non-Buddhists can practice it. The way that we make calm abiding a Buddhist practice is by being grounded in refuge in the Three Jewels and inspired by bodhicitta— the altruistic intention to achieve enlightenment for the sake of all sentient beings.

---

[14] In Tibetan cosmology, Mount Meru is the mountain at the center of the universe. Here it is being used as a metaphor for stability.

[15] Literally "middle way". The philosophical school founded by Arya Nagarjuna that espouses the wisdom understanding emptiness, free of nihilism and eternalism.

If all the many prerequisites and necessary conditions are present, it's possible to accomplish shamatha in six months. For instance, in the *Mahayanasutraalamkara Karika* (*The Ornament of Mahayana Sutras*) the ideal place for this meditation is described as 'a noble place with a noble friend.' It also says that the meditator should have assembled all the necessary ingredients, internal and external.

The most important factor in choosing a place to practice calm abiding meditation is that it be free from noise and clamor. As you know, noise is the most detrimental thing for a meditator because it interrupts one's attention. Also, if we practice this meditation for a couple of weeks, but keep breaking our meditation and socializing with our friends, then it will be very difficult for us to accomplish calm abiding.

In the context of discussion of calm abiding, we have to study the nine stages of concentration. The first step is to find a suitable object of meditation. This can be either a physical or non-physical object. An example of a non-physical object could be the mind itself. But for us, I think it's more suitable to begin with a somewhat grosser object of meditation such as our breath.

You begin by watching your breath; just becoming aware of the motion of your breath as it leaves your nostrils, and again as it reenters your nostrils. Each cycle of out-breath and in-breath counts as one. Again the air moves out, you're aware the air is moving out, and as you breathe in, you count 'two'. Do this until you can do three sets of seven without losing your attention on the breath. If you lose count, it's a sign that your mind is distracted.

In any kind of meditation that we do there are two main tools: mindfulness and alertness. Mindfulness is what keeps our mind connected to the chosen object of meditation. Alertness monitors whether or not our mind is maintaining its focus upon the chosen object. We need to continue to utilize these tools until we achieve complete mental stability.

In the beginning, it's better if we choose something small as the object of our meditation, and then expand it. For those of us who suffer from attachment it's recommended that we meditate on skeletons. In Vasubhandu's *Abhidharmakosha* (*Treasury of Knowledge*), he says you should begin this kind of meditation focusing on a small area of bare bone, such as the spot between your eyebrows. Then as your mind is able to stay focused for longer, you imagine an ever-increasing area where the skin becomes bare bone. The area of bare bone increases in size until you are able to visualize your entire body as a skeleton. When you've become competent at this visualization then you can extend it to your environment and to the people and beings in your neighborhood, until, as it says in the *Abhidharmakosha*, the entire earth is covered with bone. Then you withdraw from the outer edges of your visualization and begin to contract your field of visualization and recover the earth and its inhabitants with flesh until you are back to your original point. You then repeat the process.

In any meditation, we need to employ mindfulness and alertness to rid ourselves of laxity and excitation—two things that interfere with our meditation. In Tibetan, the term for laxity literally translates as 'sinking' and mental excitation is described as 'going wild'. Whenever these two aspects enter our meditation we have to seek appropriate antidotes. When you experience a heavy mental laxity in your meditation, one remedy is to increase the level of illumination. You can stand up from your cushion and take a little stroll back and forth. If you're meditating with eyes tightly closed and you find yourself feeling disoriented, don't open your eyes right away. Open them slowly and only partially until you can just gaze at the tip of your nose.

Many people ask, "What is meditation?" The answer is very simple. Meditation means to imagine. You can imagine all your possessions in your living room right now, meaning that you can invoke the image of them in your mind. In the same way, if you're meditating on the merit field, for example, you make a thorough and detailed examination of the thangka[16] painting or picture, and then you try to recreate that same image within your mind.

Along with shamatha, we're also seeking to accomplish vipashyana and to integrate these two aspects of meditation into one. As the author writes here: *bless me to quickly produce in my mindstream the integrated path of shamatha and vipashyana.* Attaining calm abiding alone is not enough. We have actually accomplished calm abiding many times in our past lives. Through the process of death and rebirth, however, this ability has diminished, and ultimately has been lost. There are a number of reasons for this. For example, we've taken many rebirths in the god realms of the desire realm, the seventeen realms of the form realm, and the four formless realms. To be born in any of these realms, but particularly to be born in the form or the formless realms, one must have at least attained the stage of samadhi, the prerequisite for which is having accomplished calm abiding.

Therefore, pursuing shamatha by itself isn't very effective. What we need is the combination and integration of calm abiding and penetrative insight. Then we can effectively counter our personal afflictive emotions. If you are just practicing calm abiding, it's true that you may gain a certain degree of clairvoyance or an ability to perform minor miracles, but this shouldn't be the cause for any great amazement, neither is it to be envied. Even spirits have these same powers. When we successfully minimize our personal afflictive emotions, that's the greatest miracle of all.

In ancient India there were many people who could tell the future or perform small miracles, and they were often regarded as gurus in their communities. Acharya Dharmakirti sternly dismisses that notion. In the second chapter of his *Pramanavirtika* he says, "If seeing a great distance is your measure of a guru, you'd better look for your guru among the eagles."

---

[16] A scroll painting of a holy being or object that provides visual support for a meditator's visualization.

If we wish to find the gateway to nirvana, we must follow error-free judgment in what we need to adopt and avoid. Whoever can show us these things clearly is the one who is qualified to be our teacher. If possible, our guru should be an authority on both Sutra and Tantra and be able to completely reveal both these fields. At the very least our guru should be able to impart the teaching in an authentic manner and not interject his or her personal opinion or personal applications.

Verse 10

10. *When I am well trained in the common paths*
    and have become a proper vessel
    for the Vajrayana— the pinnacle of all vehicles,
    bless me to effortlessly enter
    this gateway of all fortunate beings.

As it states clearly in this verse, the requirement for becoming a proper recipient for the practice of Vajrayana is having gone through training in the common path. The 'common path' in this verse does not refer to the preliminary practices such as 100,000 prostrations, mandala offerings, and so on. It indicates bodhicitta and the development of the wisdom understanding emptiness. The common path here stands for the Mahayana path. Mahayana has two aspects; Vajrayana (tantric vehicle) and Sutrayana (bodhisattva or perfection vehicle). These two yanas or vehicles involve the profound madhyamika view and bodhicitta. So, the author is stating that if we want to receive tantric initiation then it's essential for us to produce both the madhyamika view (wisdom of emptiness) and bodhicitta in our mindstream.

What does *and have become a proper vessel* mean? It's said that five hundred bhikshus (fully ordained monks) asked Buddha's disciple, Shariputra, to reveal to them the meaning of emptiness. Now, if someone is not mentally prepared to receive teachings on emptiness, then they won't be of any benefit, and Shariputra understood that these bhikshus were not yet suitable recipients of this teaching. So the bhikshus appealed to the bodhisattva Manjushri. Manjushri could also tell that these monks were not ready for teachings on emptiness, and he knew that if they misapprehended their meaning, they could fall either into eternalism or nihilism[17], and could even end up being reborn in one of the hells. As Arya Nagarjuna said, "In misunderstanding emptiness, those of feeble intelligence will suffer and fall, just like if you catch a snake the wrong way round you will get bitten." Yet Manjushri understood that many positive consequences could arise from the monks receiving these teachings, and with this in mind, he agreed to their request and taught them about the wisdom of emptiness.

A number of the Buddha's disciples went to him and complained that Manjushri was giving teachings to students who were not suited to receive them. Buddha replied that Manjushri was able to do this because of his high level of skill.

This verse is very appropriate for us because we are all great connoisseurs of initiations, are we not? The author explains what kind of qualifications we should have before receiving empowerments, stating that we need to become *a proper vessel* for the Vajrayana vehicle.

The line *When I am well trained in the common path* deserves our serious consideration. To generate bodhicitta we need to involve ourselves in all the practices that I mentioned before so that we can produce them in our mindstream in the form of experiential realization. We also need to penetrate the meaning of emptiness. If possible, we should have developed certain degrees of realization of both bodhicitta and the wisdom of emptiness before we receive an empowerment. In their absence we have not yet become *a proper vessel* for tantric teachings.

Many of us have taken the highest tantric initiations, and what has

---

[17] Eternalism being the belief that self and phenomena exist independently, nihilism being the belief that nothing exists in any manner at all.

become of us? If someone as highly qualified as His Holiness the Dalai Lama is bestowing the initiation, then through the power of his ability, force, and sound intentions, combined with our own understanding of the instructions he has given, perhaps we receive a certain facsimile of an initiation. If we achieve this and then amplify our understanding through meditation, and pursue the practices of the creation stage and completion stage, then we have planted a seed and good results will follow in the future. On the other hand, if one who is not a Buddhist takes an initiation, even from a highly qualified teacher, then I think that it's highly questionable whether or not the initiation is actually received. The reason for this is that in order to receive tantric vows one must have taken the bodhisattva vows, and in order to take bodhisattva vows one must take the refuge vows. So, without the foundation of the refuge vows, we cannot truly receive the higher vows.

In Buddhism, there are a number of different yanas or vehicles. The three main vehicles are Sutrayana, Mahayana, and Vajrayana. Among these vehicles, the Vajrayana is the highest. It is said that to achieve complete enlightenment, ultimately one must use the vehicle of Tantra. One cannot achieve buddhahood with the Sutra vehicle alone.

The author states that the Vajrayana is the *gateway of all fortunate beings*. The fortunate beings are individuals who have accumulated great merits. They are well trained in the common path and their minds are ready for receiving tantric initiations. The gateway is the point from where the journey begins. And then it says *bless me to effortlessly enter*, meaning that may I make this journey free of any hindrance.

It says here, *When I am well trained in the common path, and have become a proper vessel the Vajrayana—the pinnacle of all vehicles*. So, we are now ready to receive formal initiations. We enter the practice or vehicle of Tantra by first observing the bodhisattva and tantric vows and commitments (*samayas*). As it says in the next verse:

Verse 11

11. *Having discovered with unyielding conviction*
    that the ground for attaining two forms of siddhis,
    is purely observing the vows and samayas,
    bless me to safeguard these more than my life.

The purpose for receiving initiations is to accomplish the two forms of *siddhis* or powerful attainments; supreme (*chog*) and common (*thunmong*). We will not be able to accomplish these attainments without the conditions for their accomplishment.

The most essential condition for accomplishing these two forms of attainments is *purely observing the vows and samayas* or commitments.

This verse clearly tells us that it is not enough just to receive the initiation. If we don't abide by the accompanying samayas and vows we will not be able to accomplish higher goals. Some people come to the lamas and say, "I would really like to take this initiation, but please will you excuse me from the commitments?" Few of us ask, "Can I take this commitment?" or "What do these commitments mean?" We simply attend the empowerment, and afterwards we don't give it much thought. Although they may plant a seed in our minds, without the commitments, initiations are of little value. No matter what kind of vows we receive, our number one priority is learning to protect them properly.

So, in this verse, the author is telling us what our priorities should be after we have received initiations. Our core aim is the accomplishment of the two forms of powerful attainments, and to achieve this we must be in full compliance with our vows and samayas.

Verse 12

12. *Having realized the quintessential points*
    of the two stages—the heart of all Tantra,
    and unwavering from four daily yoga sessions,
    bless me to practice according to the words of the masters.

The text says *the heart of all Tantra* because there are four classes of Tantra: Kriya Tantra, Charya Tantra, Yoga Tantra and Highest Yoga Tantra. These classes of Tantra are presented in order of lowest to highest. The real heart of all these Tantras is the two stages; the creation stage and completion stage.

Having realized the quintessential points of these two stages, we make a dynamic effort in conducting four practice sessions a day: a morning session, a session before our midday meal, one in the evening and another at nighttime. We try to engage in the proper visualizations with deep concentration and without error.

Verse 13

13. *May the gurus, the beacons of the perfect path,*
    and faithfully striving companions have long life.
    May hosts of obstacles, external and internal,
    all completely subside.

This verse lists the things we wish for as practitioners. The gurus are described as *the beacons of the perfect path* meaning that they reveal to us the perfect path of both Sutra and Tantra. The striving companions are our fellow practitioners, our dharma friends who are engaged in the same practices as ourselves. So, we wish for the guru and our dharma companions to live a long time, and we seek the blessings or inspiration for the total elimination of internal and external obstacles to our practice.

An external obstacle could be an illness, a lack of resources and provisions, hostilities from other sentient beings, dangerous and threatening conditions; all things that make our practice difficult. There are also more subtle kinds of external obstacles, like when the sun is shining and the ocean is very inviting, and we choose to go to the beach instead of doing our practice, or when friends call up and say "Let's go to a movie tonight," and we rise to that invitation instead of doing our meditation. But all these external obstacles, however challenging, are minor compared to our internal ones.

Internal obstacles are our personal afflictive emotions or delusions within our mental continuum. These are the major hindrances to our dharma practice. So, when we are doing our practice, we need to find a way to counter any thought that is detrimental to our practice.

In the last line of this verse, we request that all these obstacles *completely subside*. But whom are we beseeching in all of these verses? To whom are we praying for blessings and inspiration? We're making these prayers to the objects of refuge; the Three Jewels—the Buddha, Dharma, and Sangha—that are always present with us. Every day of our lives, we must be assured that we're never separated from the Three Jewels.

I've heard some people say that they feel a sense of isolation and loneliness being a dharma student. But when you think of the refuge field, the numbers of realized beings are beyond counting. At most, you may have about twenty friends with whom you socialize, but there are numberless holy beings in the refuge field who are the best of friends to us. Then we may say, "Well, I don't see them. How do I know whether they're here or not?" In response, I'd like to offer a brief illustration.

Acharya Asanga spent a total of twelve years in retreat in a cave to accomplish the meditation on Maitreya Buddha. After three years of trying to do his practice, he felt he wasn't achieving anything. Tired and somewhat frustrated, he thought about giving up. He came out of retreat and saw a very old gentleman who was rubbing a rather large iron bar with a piece of cloth. Asanga asked the old man, "What are you doing? The old man replied, "I'm making this iron bar into a needle." Asanga thought to himself, "If this old man has the resolve and patience to make a needle out of a bar of iron, then I certainly can accomplish the realization of Maitreya Buddha," and he returned to his retreat cave.

After another three years, Asanga still couldn't see any indication that he was progressing, and again he felt discouraged. Wondering if he was ever going to achieve his goal, he rose from his meditation and left the cave. As he was coming out of his cave, he noticed a bird's nest in the mountain face. The rock had been worn into a curve by the bird's wings brushing against it on its flight to and from the nest. Asanga thought, "If feathers can carve into rock, then certainly I have a hope of accomplishing my practice of Maitreya Buddha," and he went back into retreat.

After a total of twelve years had passed, Asanga had still received no signs of success, and feeling despondent, he left his cave again. As he was walking, he came across an old female dog. In her hindquarters there was a large wound infested with maggots. The dog was unable to walk and barked aggressively at anyone who came near it. Asanga felt enormous compassion for the animal and resolved to help it in any way he could. He knew he needed to clean the wound, but he realized that if he removed the maggots they wouldn't have anything to eat and would die.

He decided that the only solution that would ensure survival for both the maggots and the dog was to find another piece of meat for the maggots to live on. Then he thought, "I don't have to go in search of meat, I have the solution right here," and he cut off a piece of his own flesh. Then he thought if he carried the maggots onto the flesh with his hands they might get crushed, and he decided that the safest thing to do was to transport them with his tongue. He put out his tongue towards the maggots and closed his eyes. But even though he kept reaching further, he couldn't feel anything. He opened his eyes to find that the dog had disappeared and Maitreya Buddha was standing in front of him.

Asanga cried out, "Oh, Maitreya! Where is your compassion? I've been seeking you for twelve years." Maitreya answered, "From the first day you entered your retreat I was there with you." Maitreya then took Asanga with him to Tushita[18] heaven for half a day, which was actually fifty years in human time. Here, Asanga received teachings from Maitreya on the *Abhisamayalamkara* (*Ornament of Clear Realization*) and the five-volume commentary of the *Prajnaparamita Sutras*.

When we think about the Three Jewels, we have to imagine them present in front of us. This is why Shakyamuni Buddha said, "Whoever thinks of me, I will immediately be there before them." If millions of practitioners simultaneously invite the Buddha to appear, then at the same moment, the Buddha will instantaneously manifest before each and every one of them.

The Buddha had a great benefactor, King Maghadha, who had a very beautiful daughter named Maghadha Zangmo. Many kings and noblemen had asked for her hand in marriage, but the king couldn't decide who would make the most suitable husband for his daughter. He asked the Buddha for advice, and the Buddha told the king that his daughter should marry a king of a small, faraway kingdom that was populated by people without any kind of spirituality.

When Maghadha Zangmo arrived at the king's palace, all the people were very happy to receive her as they'd never seen such a beautiful woman. To them she was like a goddess. After a while, however, Maghadha Zangmo found it hard to be so far away from the Buddha. Back at her home she had seen the Buddha and the sangha all the time.

---

[18] A heaven reachable through meditation where the historical Buddha resided before emanating into this world, and where Maitreya, the future Buddha, currently resides.

She became increasingly melancholy and her health began to decline. The king was concerned about her and asked, "Why do you look so unhappy? I'll give you anything you desire."

Maghadha Zangmo replied, "You have given me so much, it is really wonderful. But when I was living in my father's house I would see the Buddha and the sangha all the time, but here I can never see them."

Then the king replied, "Why don't you invite them to come, just like your father does when he gives offerings?"

This made Maghadha Zangmo very happy. "I will invite them the day after tomorrow," she said.

The king was surprised to hear this because the only transportation was by elephant. It would take one month to bring the invitation to the Buddha, and another month for him to reach the palace. When he mentioned this to Maghadha Zangmo, she just replied, "I can make the request. Buddha doesn't need a messenger."

The king knew that his wife never lied, so although he was skeptical, he set about making the arrangements. The next day, Maghadha Zangmo went to the roof of the palace, and holding some incense between her hands, she petitioned the Buddha and his entourage to come. The next day, a large gathering of people formed at the palace, curious to see what would happen. First the arhats and then the high level bodhisattvas began to arrive, traveling through the air, their feet not even touching the ground. As each of the sangha arrived, everyone asked, "Is *this* the Buddha? Is *this* the Buddha?" Then the Buddha himself arrived the same way.

When the king's subjects witnessed the power of the Buddha, it inspired tremendous faith and devotion in them and opened their minds. The Buddha gave teachings on the dharma to all who were gathered and many people gained spiritual realizations.

Even today, when we petition the Buddha and the holy beings, we recite Maghadha Zangmo's prayer.

You the protector of all sentient beings
Great Lord, you destroy all external and internal obstacles
Lord, you simultaneously know all phenomena of the three times[19]
Lord Buddha, with your retinue please come to this place.

Verse 14

14. *In all my lives may I never be apart from perfect teachers,*
    and fully enjoy the magnificent dharma.
    By attaining the complete realizations of stages and path,
    may I swiftly attain Vajradhara's state.

The first line of this verse that says *In all my lives* deserves some contemplation. This includes from this moment of our present human birth all the way through our future lives until we become a fully enlightened buddha. We are requesting to never be separated, in this and future lives, from a fully qualified spiritual teacher, and to be deeply involved in the practice of dharma.

Then the third line, *By attaining the complete realizations of stages and path.*[20] You can think of path and stages as one and the same or as aspects of one another. The stages refer specifically to the stages of meditation and the path refers to the five Mahayana paths and the ten bhumis[21] or "grounds" of the bodhisattvas.

---

[19] The three times are past, present, and future
[20] The details concerning the realizations and accomplishments of the path and its stages are explained at length in the Prajnaparamita sutras.
[21] The ten bhumis refer to the ten levels through which a bodhisattva develops, beginning with the path of seeing.

THE FIVE MAHAYANA PATHS

1. The Path of Accumulation
2. The Path of Preparation.
3. The Path of Seeing
   (the first of the ten grounds of the bodhisattva falls between 3.
   the path of seeing and 4. the path of meditation)
4. The Path of Meditation.
5. The Path of No More Learning—the state of buddhahood.

The ten bodhisattva bhumis are interlaced between the path of seeing and the path of no more learning. Generally speaking, the Buddhist path includes three sets of five paths: the five paths of shravakas (hearers), the five paths of pratyekabuddhas (solitary realizers) and the five paths of bodhisattvas. The pratyekabuddha arhat has one hundred years more accumulation of merit than the shravaka arhat. This is a vast area of discussion that I can only briefly touch upon here. When you reach the Path of No More Learning of a shravaka or pratyekabuddha, then you become an arhat or "foe destroyer", which means that you have destroyed all your afflictive emotions. This means that all the suffering and its causes have been eradicated. Once they become arhats, shravakas and pratyekabuddhas do not need to return to samsara. Yet although they have eliminated all the delusory obscurations, they have still not overcome the subtle cognitive obscurations. To achieve this they need to enter the Mahayana path.

When it comes to the Mahayana we can speak of the five paths and the ten bhumis or 'grounds.' According to the sutras, Avalokiteshvara and Manjushri are bodhisattvas of the tenth bhumi, or tenth level, which means that they are on the verge of becoming buddhas. So, these bodhisattvas who are at the last stages are called "final stream-enterers" meaning that they are in the final stream or final stage of being a sentient being.[22] They are on the uninterrupted path of the final state of meditative equipoise (Tib: *nyamshag*).

Cognitive obscurations can be broken down into ten different grades, each one more subtle than the next. The uninterrupted path of the final state of meditative equipoise counters the subtlest of those cognitive obscurations. It is described as uninterrupted because there is no break between the stage of the final stream-enterer and buddhahood itself. The moment that a tenth level bodhisattva arises from the state of meditative equipoise, he or she arises as a buddha. When one becomes a buddha, one achieves the four kayas or four bodies of a buddha.[23] These are svabhavikakaya (the natural body), dharmakaya (wisdom body), sambhogakaya (enjoyment body) and nirmanakaya (emanation body).

In terms of their realizations and accomplishments all buddhas are equal. Some people may think that some meditational deities have greater realizations or possess more qualities than others. Such thoughts should never enter our minds.

When we speak of the realizations of a buddha, we talk in terms of the mental obscurations they've eradicated as well as in terms of the realizations they've gained. As it says in the *Abidharmakosha*, when buddhas manifest on earth they may be different from the point of view of ordinary people in terms of their social status, race, body size, and lifespan, but otherwise they are the same. All buddhas possess the same knowledge, the same wisdom and the same realizations. For instance, Shakyamuni Buddha was born into the royal caste, whereas it is said that the fifth buddha, Maitreya, will come as a brahmin.[24] Also,

---

[22] If someone is a sentient being then he or she cannot be a buddha because a buddha is not a sentient being.

[23] Sometimes three kayas or bodies of a buddha are counted instead of four. They are: dharmakaya, sambhogakaya, and nirmanakaya.

[24] In Indian society, a priest or scholar of the highest caste.

the life-spans of buddhas can vary. Shakyamuni Buddha lived for eighty-two years, but it is said that Maitreya Buddha will live for eighty thousand years.

When we arise from the state of meditative equipoise having eradicated all the delusions and cognitive obscurations, the pureness of having eradicated these elements is the svabhavikakaya or natural buddha body. The dharmakaya or the wisdom body is that radiant mind that is now rid of all obstacles and contaminations. The dharmakaya arises pure, radiant, and omniscient, comprehending all phenomena. The nirmanakaya is related with the thirty-two major and eighty minor signs of buddhahood. These are the physical signs by which one can recognize a buddha. They are listed as one of a buddha's 'five certainties' or defining characteristics, which relate to the sambhogakaya.

1. The certainty of physical appearance is having the thirty-two major and eighty minor physical signs.
2. The certainty of time is remaining until the very end of cyclic existence.
3. The certainty of dharma is always giving discourses on the Mahayana.
4. The certainty of students is surrounding themselves with disciples such as arya bodhisattvas.
5. The certainty of place is continuing to abide in Akanishta Pure Land.

The nirmanakya is translated as 'emanation body,' so from where does it emanate? It emanates from the sambhogakaya or enjoyment body, which originates from the dharmakaya. Maitreya Buddha is presently residing in the form of sambhogakaya and will eventually arrive as nirmanakaya or emanation body on this earth.

This concludes the complete teaching on the foundation of all excellences. It is my hope that it is of some use for you. However, I know from personal experience that it is extremely difficult to retain everything we have discussed. But whatever you are able to retain, I appeal to you to try to translate that into practice.

Now I'd like to offer a list of four points that I consider important.

1. It is far more important to practice the dharma than to have knowledge of the dharma.
2. Between self and others, others are more important.
3. Between the meaning and the word, the meaning is of more importance.
4. Between this life and our future lives, our future lives are more important.

When we practice the dharma, we must begin with the proper motivation. During our practice we should maintain good concentration, and at the end of our practice we should do the proper dedication.

Good at the Beginning

When we practice, listen to teachings, or teach the dharma, we must not be motivated by the eight worldly concerns. Our dharma practice should be aimed towards being freed from samsara and delusions.

Good in the Middle

During our practice or while we are listening to teachings, we should pay careful attention. We shouldn't be like an upside down pot in which nothing can enter. Again, our motivation should be pure, because otherwise our mind is like a dirty pot and our practice will be contaminated.

Good at the End

Making the proper dedication at the end of our practice or after we've finished listening to teachings is also very important. If we dedicate the merit so that in our future lives we can enjoy success in our dharma practice, then that is good. If we dedicate the merit to be free of samsara that is even better. And if we include others in that aspiration and wish for us all to become fully enlightened, that is the highest form of dedication and the proper dedication for Mahayana practitioners. We should think, *'By the power of these positive actions, may we all become buddhas'*.

Arya Nagarjuna said that just like the bridle controls the direction of your horse, the quality of your dedication determines the results that come from your spiritual actions.

Dedication of Merit

L ET US DEDICATE our positive energy to the flourishing of Buddha-dharma throughout the world.

Let us dedicate our positive energy to the long life of His Holiness the Dalai Lama. May his sacred mandalas of body, speech, and mind be unharmed by negative intentions and actions. May he and other great masters be successful in fulfilling their dreams and visions for benefiting all sentient beings.

Let us dedicate our positive energy to all spiritual communities throughout the world, so that they may flourish in their study, contemplation and meditation.

Let us dedicate our positive energy to the elimination of the problems in our world, such as famine, war and conflict. May everyone in this and other world systems experience peace, happiness and harmony.

Let us dedicate our positive energy to ourselves and to other dharma practitioners, so that we may overcome all obstacles to spiritual development.

Let us dedicate our positive energy to ourselves and to all sentient beings, so that we can purify the obscurations to liberation and omniscience and quickly reach full enlightenment.

Question & Answer

Student 1: For my spiritual practice, for refuge, for thinking of going to enlightenment, the motivation that comes with fear is very difficult.

Geshe Gyeltsen: Do you have no fear?

Student 1: I do have fear.

Geshe Gyeltsen: If you have fear then you have one of the two excellent causes for refuge. When you experience this fear you should ask yourself, "Who can help me?" Think about it. If the hell realms or the hungry ghost realms don't exist, that's great news, right? That's wonderful. But in case such places do exist, then it's our job to take precautions. Certainly, we can't have total confidence that we won't find ourselves in such places in our next life. Even if we don't end up in a lower realm in our next life, if our thoughts about these realms lead us to seek the protection and companionship of the Three Jewels, then I think that serves us well.

But fear is not the only driving force behind our practice. We also witness the sufferings of other sentient beings and this motivates us to practice. If fear is not the major motivator for your dharma practice then I compliment you. There are many other reasons to engage in dharma that we discover later.

Student 1: I have a hard time being present with the fear when it arises.

Geshe Gyeltsen: Then you should think about all other sentient beings. Don't think about yourself. Think that you're doing this for others. We need to know both the positive and negative side of things if we want to be freed from the negative. If we don't know or think about the negative side, we will be unable to move from that state.

Student 2: Is enlightenment only accessible through Buddhism?

Geshe Gyeltsen: I think that if another faith describes the progression on the path and stages that Buddhism lays out and if these teachings are accessible, then certainly you don't necessarily need to be a Buddhist to be enlightened. But if another faith doesn't explain each step of the path from the beginning and give an explanation of enlightenment, then I think we need Buddhism. If there's no road it's very difficult to travel by car because rocks and boulders will obstruct our way. Buddhism provides that road and also teaches us what to do when we come across a boulder so that we can continue on the journey.

Glossary

Skt. = Sanskrit

Tib. = Tibetan

acharya (Skt.). A prominent teacher and scholar who teaches by his/her own example. Often added to a person's name as a title of respect.

arhat (Skt.). One who has gone beyond rebirth in cyclic existence.

arya (Skt.). Noble being; one who has realized the path of direct insight into the way things truly exist.

Asanga (5th c.). Indian scholar who founded the Cittamatra or Mind-Only school.

Atisha (982-1054). Indian *mahasiddha* who revitalized Buddhism in Tibet and founded the Kadam tradition. Author of the *Lamp for the Path to Enlightenment*.

Avalokiteshvara (Skt.). Male meditational deity embodying fully enlightened compassion. Often pictured with 1,000 arms.

bardo (Tib.). Literally "intermediate state" or "in-between state". The state of existence between two lives—after death and before one's next birth, when one's consciousness is not connected with a physical body.

bhikshu (Skt.). A male renunciant in the Buddhist order; monk.

bhumi (Skt.). Literally, ground; level on the bodhisattva path

bodhicitta (Skt.). The "thought of enlightenment"; the determination to attain enlightenment for the benefit of sentient beings. There are two types: relative and ultimate. Relative bodhicitta is further classified into two types: aspiring and engaging bodhicitta.

bodhisattva (Skt.). One who truly generates bodhicitta.

buddha (Skt.). Enlightened or fully awakened one; a being who has completely abandoned all obscurations and has perfected every good quality.

Buddhadharma. The teachings of the historical Buddha Shakyamuni.

buddhahood. See enlightenment

calm-abiding. A meditative state of one-pointed focus; quietude.

celestial god (Skt. *deva*). A type of being who enjoys the highest pleasures to be found in cyclic existence but who is afflicted with pride.

cyclic existence. See *samsara.*

Dalai Lama. The temporal and spiritual leader of Tibet, recognized as the human embodiment of Avalokiteshvara, the bodhisattva of compassion.

deva (Skt.). See *celestial god.*

dharma (Skt.). A term with many shades of meaning, generally referring to the teachings of Buddhism but which can also refer to the realizations that result from practicing the teachings.

Dharmakirti. Influential 7th century teacher and scholar at India's Nalanda University.

Dromtönpa. Tibetan scholar and main student of Atisha.

emptiness. See *shunyata*

enlightenment (Skt. *bodhi*). Full enlightenment; buddhahood; the ultimate goal of Buddhist practice attained when all limitations have been removed from the mind and all one's positive potential has been realized; a state characterized by unlimited compassion, skill, and wisdom.

four immeasurables. Immeasurable love, compassion, joy and equanimity.

Hevajra (Skt.). One of the Mahanuttarayoga Tantras.

Hinayana (Skt.). The "lesser vehicle" or "individual vehicle" as opposed to the "great vehicle" of the Mahayana. The practitioners on this vehicle strive for their own individual liberation, or the state of an *arhat.*

Kadam. Tradition of Tibetan Buddhism founded by Atisha.

karma (Skt.). Action; the working of cause and effect whereby positive actions produce happiness and negative actions produce suffering; the impression or seed that an action leaves on one's mental continuum, which must eventually ripen and produce a result.

kaya. (Skt.). The 'body' of a buddha, the term refers to the different dimensions in which a Buddha's attributes reside.

lam-rim (Tib.). "Stages of the Path to Enlightenment"; a reformulation of Shakyamuni Buddha's words into a complete and integrated system of practice, which outline the practices leading to great enlightenment.

Madhyamika (Skt.). "Middle Way" refers to the doctrine of emptiness that avoids the two extremes of eternalism (that things exist independently) and nihilism (that nothing exists at all).

mahasiddha (Skt.). A greatly accomplished tantric practitioner.

Mahayana (Skt.). The "great vehicle"; the path of those seeking enlightenment with the motivation to liberate all beings from suffering and its causes and to establish them in complete enlightenment.

Maitreya (Skt.). The next buddha to come once Shakyamuni Buddha's teachings have disappeared from the world.

mandala. (Skt.). A symbolic representation of the universe; the abode of a meditational deity as the emanation of that deity; one's personal surroundings as a reflection of one's state of mind.

Manjushri (Skt.). Male meditational deity embodying fully enlightened wisdom.

Marpa. (1012-1097). One of the greatest Tibetan translators and the founder of the Kagyu school of Tibetan Buddhism.

Milarepa (1040-1123). Great Tibetan saint, and chief disciple of Marpa.

Mount Meru. Giant mountain at the center of the world system and the mandala offering.

Nagarjuna. Indian mahasiddha who elucidated the Perfection of Wisdom Sutras of Shakyamuni Buddha and founded the Madhyamika school of philosophy.

Naropa (11th c.). A great Indian yogi, chief disciple of Tilopa and teacher of Marpa.

nirvana (Skt.). The state of complete liberation from samsara in which all mental delusions have been overcome and one is permanently free from all suffering; the goal of the practitioner seeking his or her own freedom from suffering.

omniscience. The quality of a buddha's mind which signifies complete knowledge of all reality.

paramita (Skt.). See *perfections.*

perfections. The six "transcending" practices of the Mahayana path, which define the bodhisattva's way of life: 1) generosity; 2) ethics; 3) patience; 4) enthusiastic perseverance; 5) concentration; 6) wisdom.

prajna (Skt.) true insight into the realization of emptiness. Combined with skilful means and great compassion, prajna leads to the attainment of full enlightenment.

Prajnaparamita. Literally "Perfection of Wisdom". The genre of Buddhist texts dealing with emptiness. Can also refer to the last of the six perfections of a bodhisattva.

pratimoksha. The practice of ethical discipline which lays the foundation for a person's eventual liberation from cyclic existence.

pratyekabudhha (Skt.). "Solitary realizer"; higher of the two types of Hinayana arhats, who attains nirvana without needing teachings in that lifetime, but lacks the complete realization of a buddha and thus cannot help other sentient beings as much as a buddha can.

pure land. Environments which are totally free from mental and physical suffering and which are associated with a particular buddha.

refuge. In Buddhism, a formal commitment of entrusting one's spiritual wellbeing to the Three Jewels: the Buddha, the Dharma and the Sangha, as the essential aspects of the path to enlightenment. See *Three Jewels.*

Renunciation. A mental attitude that is free from clinging to worldly things and pleasures combined with the aspiration towards the path to freedom from suffering.

samadhi (Skt.). A profound meditative state in which the mind is fully concentrated on a single object.

samaya (Skt.). A sacred commitment or pledge taken by a practitioner as a prerequisite for the practice of Tantra.

samsara (Skt.). Cyclic existence; the repetitive cycle of death and rebirth characterized by suffering and fueled by ignorance and contaminated karma.

sangha (Skt.). Monastic community following the teachings of the Buddha; the assembly of noble beings on the path to liberation and enlightenment; spiritual friends who help us in our practice of the dharma.

Shakyamuni Buddha (563-483 BC). Fourth of the 1000 founding buddhas of this present world age; born a prince of the Shakya clan in North India; founder of what came to be known as Buddhism.

shamatha (Skt.). See *calm abiding.*

Shantideva. Indian scholar and yogi; author of the classic text, *Bodhicarya-vatara.*

Shariputra. One of the two main disciples of the historical Buddha who became an arhat renowned for his wisdom.

shastra. (Skt.). Authentic commentary that elucidates the meaning of the Buddha's teachings.

sentient being. Any being having a consciousness who has not yet attained buddhahood.

shravaka (Skt.). Literally "hearer" or "listener"; one who has achieved liberation from cyclic existence on the Hinayana path mainly with the help of a spiritual guide.

shunyata (Skt.). Voidness or emptiness; the true nature of reality characterized by the absence of any independent, self-existence in persons or things.

siddhi (Skt.). Spiritual power or psychic ability. Includes simple forms of clairvoyance to being able to levitate, be present at various places at once, become as small as an atom, materialize objects, have access to memories from past lives, etc.

six perfections. See *perfections.*

sutra (Skt.). A discourse of Shakyamuni Buddha; the pre-tantric division of Buddhist teachings stressing the scriptural texts and the teachings they contain.

Sutrayana. Vehicle of the sutra teachings, the discourses taught by the historical Buddha.

Tantra (Skt.). Advanced meditational practices and their accompanying texts not taught in the sutras. Tantra focuses on the practice of deity yoga, which has the potential to quickly lead a practitioner to complete enlightenment; also *Tantrayana.*

Tara. A female buddha and meditational deity of enlightened activity and fearlessness.

tathagata (Skt.). A buddha, a perfectly realized one.

ten bhumis. See *bhumi*

thangka (Tib.) A scroll painting of a holy being or object that provides visual support for a meditator's visualization.

three baskets. (Skt. tripitaka). The Buddhist canon which falls into three categories: the Vinaya (the code of ethics), the sutras (Buddha's discourses), and the abhidharma (the systemized philosophical and psychological analysis of existence that is the basis of Buddhist systems of tenets and mind training.

Three Jewels. The Buddha, the Dharma and Sangha; the teacher who manifests enlightened qualities, the teachings and realizations, and the spiritual companions who assist practitioners on the path to enlightenment.

tonglen (Tib.). Literally "giving and receiving"; the meditation on receiving the suffering of others and giving them happiness.

Tsongkhapa, Lama (1357-1419). Founder of the Gelug tradition of Tibetan Buddhism; revitalized many Sutra and Tantra lineages as well as the monastic tradition in Tibet.

Vajrayana (Skt.) See *Tantra.*

Vasubandhu. Indian scholar and author of *Abhidharmakosha.*

vinaya (Skt.) See *three baskets.*

vipashyana (Skt.). Special insight. An analytical meditative state penetrating the nature of reality and based upon the practice of calm abiding.

wheel of life. The repetitive cycle of birth and rebirth in unenlightened existence symbolized as a wheel divided into six realms.

wisdom. The discriminative awareness that understands the true nature of reality; can also refer to the natural awareness of the mind of a buddha.

yana (Skt.). Literally "vehicle"; any path to enlightenment.

yidam (Skt.). Meditational deity

⁙ About the Author

GESHE TSULTIM GYELTSEN was born in 1924 in the Kham province of eastern Tibet. His parents named him Jamphel Yeshe and at a young age he was inspired by the example of his uncle who was a monk at the local monastery. When the boy was only seven, he and his family decided that he would enter monastic life. For nine years he studied Sutra and Tantra and received teachings on dialectics under the tutelage of Geshe Jampa Thaye, a highly respected teacher from Sera Monastery.

When he was sixteen, Geshe Gyeltsen decided to continue his studies and left for Lhasa, the capital of Tibet, to study for his geshe degree at Sera Monastery. The geshe degree in the Gelug school is comparable to a western doctorate in Buddhist philosophy. The difference is that a geshe degree usually takes more than twenty years to complete.

Geshe Gyeltsen set out on the thirty-three day trek across twenty-five mountain passes, the only monk in a party of fifteen merchants and pilgrims. When they had almost reached Lhasa, they stopped near Gaden Monastery where some monks invited him to join them for tea the following day. The next morning as he climbed the hill toward Gaden, Geshe Gyeltsen saw the great monastery for the first time looking as though it would touch the sky. He wept tears of joy and knew without question that it was here, and not Sera, where he would continue his studies. That day was the anniversary of Lama Tsongkhapa's enlightenment. In the evening, the light offerings of butter lamps and the sound of chanting filled every room in the monastery and Geshe Gyeltsen felt deeply moved by its spiritual atmosphere.

He joined Shartse College, one of Gaden's two main colleges. The abbot at that time was the late Kyabje Zong Rinpoche who took a special interest in the young monk's progress. Geshe Gyeltsen studied logic, wisdom, compassion, ethics, phenomenology, and mind training at Gaden for twenty years and later became a teacher of junior monks.

After the Tibetan Uprising of March 10th, 1959, word reached Gaden that His Holiness the Dalai Lama had left Tibet. Geshe Gyeltsen and a group of six other monks left the monastery after evening prayers and made their way to India across the Himalayas; members of a mass exodus fleeing the oppression of the Chinese Communist occupation. He was one of the few senior monks who managed to escape out of the twenty thousand monks that had lived at Gaden, Sera, and Drepung: Tibet's three largest monasteries.

Geshe Gyeltsen, with fifty of the most highly regarded monks from each monastery, resettled at Dalhousie in northern India where he studied for two more years before taking his final geshe examinations. These exams were attended by masters from all schools of Tibetan Buddhism. The last week of his exams took place in Dharamsala where he engaged in rigorous debates under the scrutiny of His Holiness the Dalai Lama and his two senior tutors, the late Kyabje Ling Rinpoche and the late Kyabje Trijang Rinpoche. He passed with honors and was awarded the highest degree of Geshe Lharam.

In 1963, Geshe Gyeltsen traveled to Sussex, England, to teach at the Pestalozzi International Children's Village. He arrived with twenty-two Tibetan children who were mostly orphans or the children of parents still living in Tibet. For seven years he instructed these children in Tibetan writing, grammar, culture, and Buddhist philosophy.

Geshe Gyeltsen came to the United States in 1976 and briefly held positions at USC, at UC Santa Barbara, and at UCLA, where he taught meditation and Tibetan language. His university students requested that he start a teaching center, and in 1978 he founded a center for the study of Buddhism in Los Angeles. He requested His Holiness the Dalai Lama to name the center and His Holiness gave the name of Thubten Dhargye Ling, which means Land of Flourishing Dharma.

Thubten Dhargye Ling is now based in Long Beach where Geshe Gyeltsen offers classes in meditation, holds retreats, celebrates religious holidays and gives regular teachings from traditional Buddhist texts. His teachings are archived on the Internet and are broadcast live over the web at www.tdling.com.

Geshe Gyeltsen has founded centers in Northern California, Colorado, Texas, Mexico City and Denmark, and has students based around the world. He is also involved in various humanitarian projects in India, including the construction of an Indian School for the Blind, a classroom and playground for an Indian school, and a home for Gaden Monastery's elderly monks. He also funds a Tibetan Elders Home, provides meals for schoolchildren, and helps to fund various educational programs. These programs include the training of Tibetan educators and the education of monks and nuns arriving from Tibet. He also actively works for human rights and true autonomy for the Tibetan people.

Geshe Gyeltsen is known for his great compassion and personal warmth while retaining a traditional and uncompromising approach to teaching the dharma. His strength of vision and devotion to his practice transcend time and culture, and he continues to inspire his students with the legacy he has brought from Tibet.

Other books by Geshe Tsultim Gyeltsen:
Keys to Great Enlightenment (TDL Publications, 2006)
Mirror of Wisdom: Teachings on Emptiness (TDL Publications, 2000)

Other TDL books:
Illuminating the Path to Enlightenemnt by His Holiness the Dalai Lama (TDL Publications, 2002)

Interested persons may contact Thubten Dhargye Ling by calling (562) 621-9865, emailing office@tdling.com, or by writing to 3500 East 4th St. Long Beach, CA 90814. Visit the website at www.tdling.com.

LAMA TSONGKHAPA was one of the greatest spiritual masters of Tibet and is considered to have been an emanation of the bodhisattva of wisdom, Manjushri. Lama Tsongkhapa studied under teachers of all traditions and became a very learned scholar as well as an accomplished yogi. He was a prolific writer, creating eighteen volumes of work on the dharma. The founder of the Gelug school of Tibetan Buddhism, Lama Tsongkhapa emphasized pure ethical discipline as the basis for spiritual development.

LOSANG GYALTSEn translated the oral commentary of Lama Tsong-khapa's *The Foundation of All Good Qualities* from Tibetan into English. He is a graduate of Sanskrit University's Institute of Higher Tibetan Studies in Varanasi, India, and has worked as a translator for the Library of Tibetan Works and Archives.

A Note About Dharma Books

Books containing dharma teachings or the images of dharma teachers are very precious because they represent the teachings and beings that can lead us to full enlightenment. This is a reason to treat dharma books with respect. According to tradition, we do not put dharma books, or any other dharma literature, on the floor or underneath other things, step over or sit on them, or use them for mundane purposes. They are kept in a clean, high place, separate from worldly writings.

10.31.07